The Techniques of
Painted Attic Pottery

JOSEPH VEACH NOBLE

The Techniques of Painted Attic Pottery

Revised Edition

with 278 illustrations, 12 in colour

THAMES AND HUDSON

Dedicated to Dietrich von Bothmer
distinguished scholar, mentor, and friend

Published with the assistance and cooperation of the J. Paul Getty Museum
© 1988 Thames & Hudson Ltd, London

Printed and bound in the German Democratic Republic

CONTENTS

PREFACE

OVER FORTY YEARS have elapsed since the publication of the book *The Craft of Athenian Pottery* by Gisela M. A. Richter in 1923, and, although it has been long out of print, the book continues to be useful. Most of the content of the book remains valid today, and I gratefully acknowledge the standards and guidance Miss Richter established. In particular, many of the references to ancient literature which I use are based on her comprehensive chapter on the subject. Before writing her book, Miss Richter engaged in the actual practice of making pottery and experienced the difficulties of throwing, turning, and firing vases. She felt that to understand fully the techniques of the craft, it was necessary to master them; this is still an essential approach.

The techniques used to produce Attic pottery have long intrigued scholars, but only in the past two and a half decades has important progress been made in analyzing and reproducing them. The turning point in the technical study was the reproduction of the ancient black glaze in 1942 by Dr Theodor Schumann.

There remains ample material for further study in the techniques of Attic pottery.[1] First, in the field of the pottery techniques used to form the vases. Second, in the field of the accessory colors or colored clay slips. Third, in the technical analysis of the black glaze. Fourth, in the discovery of the means by which the Greek painters applied their black glaze and accessory colors to the vases, including the proper sequence of this process. Fifth, in the reproduction of the technique of making the celebrated Attic relief line, which, though studied, had never been successfully reproduced.[2]

This study is mainly concerned with the techniques of Attic pottery of the black-figure and the red-figure styles, the period from the late seventh to the late fourth century BC. It is the era which constitutes the high point in the exercise of Attic ceramic skill and attainment. In addition, however, I have included some studies of other periods and cultures, from the Egyptian black and red ware of the third millennium BC to the Barbotine pottery of the

Roman period as late as the fourth century A D, wherever they have bearing on the techniques of Attic painted pottery. I have made no attempt to be comprehensive other than in the selected time, although in it a broad span of pottery techniques can be studied.

I wish to express my gratitude to Sir John Beazley for his encouragement and suggestions in the early work on this project. Mr G. Roger Edwards of the University Museum, Philadelphia, was most helpful in the field of Hellenistic pottery and the Barbotine technique. Mr. H. M. Allred and Mr P. H. Lewis of the Texaco Research Center, Beacon, New York, made the photomicrographs and the x-ray diffraction examinations of Attic clay and pottery samples.

My thanks are also due to several of my colleagues at The Metropolitan Museum of Art for their assistance. The late Mr Murray Pease, Conservator, was invaluable in his technical counsel. Mr Fong Chow, Associate Curator of Far Eastern Art, has given good advice based on a professional potter's knowledge. Mr William Pons, Manager of the Photographic Studio, personally made many of the photographs that illustrate this book, including the series on the production of the kylix. Miss Carolyn L. Richardson worked with untiring care on the manuscript.

In the Department of Greek and Roman Art, Brian F. Cook, Associate Curator, and Andrew Oliver, Jr, Assistant Curator, conferred with me on many points. Miss Marjorie J. Milne, formerly Research Associate, contributed the appendix on the translation and analysis of the ancient poem, "Kiln." Lastly, Dr Dietrich von Bothmer, Curator of Greek and Roman Art, a valued friend, has very kindly given extensive assistance, guidance, and direction, and has reviewed the entire manuscript. He unreservedly placed at my disposal his personal notes and photographs which have immeasurably helped this publication. It was because of my many discussions with him about the techniques of Attic pottery and our collaboration on various ceramic problems that I undertook this study.

New York, 1965   J. V. N.

PREFACE TO THE REVISED EDITION

MUCH HAS HAPPENED in the field of Greek vase studies since the original publication of this book more than twenty years ago. During this time there has occurred the death of a number of scholars who made important contributions to the subject. In particular I note with sorrow the passing of three whose work greatly assisted me: the incomparable Sir John Beazley who made the study of Greek vases a distinctive discipline; Gisela M. A. Richter, a scholar with a very practical turn of mind; and Marjorie J. Milne, the gentle exacting philologist.

The technical study of Greek vases was greatly enhanced by the international symposium, Ancient Greek and Related Pottery, held in Amsterdam 12–15 April 1984, and the subsequent excellent publication of the proceedings.[3] The project was carried out by J. M. Hemelrijk and H. A. G. Brijder at the Allard Pierson Museum.

Other events of importance which also expanded the field of study were two major traveling exhibitions in the United States, "The Art of South Italy: Vases from Magna Graecia," and "The Amasis Painter and His World." The former was created by Margaret Ellen Mayo of the Virginia Museum in 1982, and the latter by Dietrich von Bothmer of The Metropolitan Museum of Art in 1985. Definitive catalogs were published for both exhibitions.[4,5] The South Italian project recognized the life work of Arthur Dale Trendall.

A number of the vases illustrated in *The Techniques of Painted Attic Pottery* formerly were in my personal collection. Now they are in the permanent collection of the Tampa Museum of Art, Florida.[6]

The first edition of this book was published in 1965 by Watson-Guptill Publications, New York, in co-operation with The Metropolitan Museum of Art. This revised edition has been produced by Thames and Hudson Ltd, London, with the assistance of the J. Paul Getty Museum. My sincere thanks go to all who have made this publication possible.

Maplewood, N.J. 1988   J. V. N.

INTRODUCTION

THE POTTERY OF ancient Athens, now scattered throughout the world, stands as a witness to an era of perfection in the union of technique and beauty. Our admiration for Attic vases matches that of the ancients: Athenaeus quotes the poet Kritias in his *Deipnosophistae*, I, 28, c: "But the city which sets up her fair trophy at Marathon devised the potter's wheel and the offspring of clay and kiln, pottery most renowned, useful about the house." Athenaeus then comments: "And Attic pottery is in fact highly esteemed."[1]

Potter and painter

In the making of pottery the work divides itself readily into three areas of skill: the forming, decorating, and the firing. Sometimes a potter decorated his own wares, but usually there was a division of these two labors. The relation of the potter to the vase-painter in ancient Athens has been discussed by Sir John Beazley.[2] Usually the potter owned and operated the kiln, and he needed the services of several vase-painters to decorate his output.[3] The tendency was for a potter and his vase-painters to form a working team, and for this arrangement to continue as long as harmony prevailed and the quality of each man's contribution remained satisfactory. It is questionable whether two potters could collaborate in making one vase; possibly one could have thrown the vase, and the other turned and refined its shape in the finishing operation. In rare instances, two painters did work on the same vase. The reason for this collaboration is not clear – perhaps it was the result of mass production – but the evidence is unmistakable. One example is a large red-figured loutrophoros in The University Museum in Philadelphia. The principal painter was the Achilles Painter; however, on the same vase, a small frieze on the body as well as figures on the neck are by the Sabouroff Painter.[4] In similar collaborative pieces, the painter's working companions or apprentices are revealed.

Signatures

Signatures occur on some vases – either painted on before firing or incised. Sometimes the signature is that of the potter followed by the word *epoiesen*, meaning "made it." If the painter signed, his name is followed by the word *egrapsen* or "painted it." Double signatures are usually "X made it, Y painted it," thus "Hieron made it, Makron painted it." This type of signature recognizes the sequence of work and the equal importance of the potting and the painting. A few vases are signed "X made and painted it," showing the dual skill of a single worker such as Exekias. Occasionally, the roles changed over the years. Euphronios began as both a potter and a painter; later he stopped painting and only formed the pots. Possibly this resulted from failing eyesight, an affliction which would not have hindered him as a potter. Unfortunately, the practice of signing was not consistent, nor was it practiced by all the potters or painters. Many of the best craftsmen never signed their work, and others did so only sporadically. A fine painter might sign an indifferent piece and omit his name on a masterpiece. Therefore, the reason for signing is obscure. It has been thought that in some cases a potter's signature might only signify his position as the owner of the pottery. Duplication of craftsmen's names and the possibility of the signing of another's name has led to some ambiguity.[5]

In the final analysis, the characteristic qualities of the workmanship truly identify the unsigned work of the potters and painters whose names are lacking. Names have been given to these unidentified workmen for the sake of classification by those who have studied and compiled their individual output.[6]

A careful study of vase shapes permits the assignment of a series of similar vases to the same potter.[7] For example, the style and idiosyncrasies of one potter's work on lekythoi allow his pottery to be grouped together. However, this type of comparison is no help if we want to attribute a group of amphorae to the same potter. A study of pottery forms by Brian F. Cook indicates that at least three potters in succession produced lekythoi which were decorated by the Berlin Painter. Beazley has shown that the potter Kachrylion made cups for at least ten different vase-painters, as did the potter Euphronios. Names assigned to potters are sometimes indicative of the style of their work. For instance, the Potter of the Heavy Hydriae is so named because his work does not show an appreciation of the more delicate problems of balanced rhythm in his outline; his forms tend to be thick and massive.

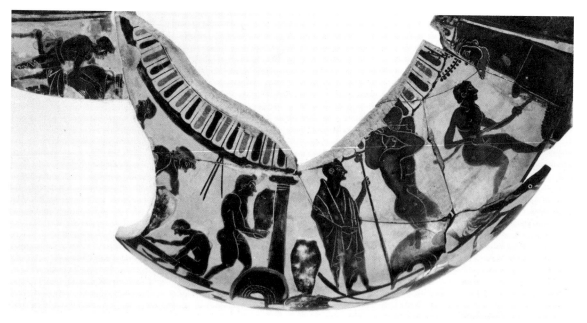

1 Hydria, by the Painter of the Leagros Group, showing a pottery in operation. Some workers are involved with the forming and throwing of the pots; others are loading them into the kiln for firing. See also ills. 6 and 230.

Workshop

The size of the potters' workshops in ancient Athens probably varied greatly as ours do today. Undoubtedly, there was the tiny shop of the poor or highly independent potter who shared his labors with only his wheel-turning apprentice. These labors were many and varied; they included mining and purifying the clay, wedging it, throwing the vases on the wheel, joining sections, turning and finishing operations, decorating the vases, obtaining wood or charcoal for the kiln, firing the kiln, and selling the finished merchandise. The successful pottery owner most likely staffed his large workshop with a variety of laborers, semiskilled and skilled artisans, and probably he himself served as the foreman or supervisor. This is clearly shown in ill. 1.[8] If the subject on the vase shown in ill. 2[9] is to be taken as an actual illustration it reveals that occasionally women worked in a pottery. Probably some Attic potteries employed as many as a dozen workers. However, the average number of employees would have been from four to six.

1,2

Economics

The economics of successfully supporting and operating these industrial enterprises leads me to believe that it is possible to determine realistic ancient sale prices of Attic pottery. Many of the price references to vases in ancient inscriptions and literature, as well as the price *graffiti* on the feet of certain vases, are misleading and inconclusive.[10] Based on the standard wage of one drachma per day in Athens in the late fifth century BC, as was paid to the skilled workers on the Erechtheum, and applying a modern cost accounting method of estimating daily production and expenses including labor and the cost of raw materials, the following prices may approximate those charged in ancient Athens. A red-figured hydria of average size would have sold for about 4 drachmas,[11] a medium-size kylix for 2–3 drachmas, a small skyphos for 1 drachma, and a very small low-quality lekythos for 1 obol.[12] Although costs estimated in this manner can never be exact, they should be close to the actual price. Therefore, the literary evidence of inscriptions, *graffiti*, and the like, can be tested against the estimated prices to ascertain whether this literary evidence is reasonable and applicable. These figures can be transposed into modern prices by equating 1 drachma to the amount of a modern wage for one day.

As in all businesses, competition was keen and potters tried to outdo their rivals. One vase-painter, Euthymides, joyfully boasted in an inscription that he painted on a vase: "Never has Euphronios painted the like of this."[13] The constant friendly rivalry to surpass the efforts of other workers had its favorable influence on the continuous development of the pottery. Of course, the economic aspects of the competition did cause some bitter feelings. This struggle was noted by Aristotle in his *Rhetoric*, 2, 4, 21, 22: "[We are friendly

2 Hydria, by the Leningrad Painter, with a scene of an idealized representation of a vase-painter's workshop. Four painters are shown: a man, two youths, and a woman. Athena and two nikai are about to crown with laurel the heads of the three male vase-painters, apparently to reward them for their excellent work. See Chapter 3, note 11, for detailed description; also ill. 206.

towards] our equals, and towards those who have the same interests, if they do not clash with us, and if their livelihood does not come from the same source, for thus arises the proverb 'Potter hates potter.'"

The potters and painters were craftsmen engaged in a hard but honest trade. They took their place among the other artisans and tradespeople who made the products and performed the services that were required for the business life of Athens. In his *Lexicon*, Suidas records a popular saying: "'To make pottery'; commonly said instead of 'to work hard.'"

The growth of Athens and the development of its foreign exports increased the demand for fine Attic pottery. Perhaps as many as a hundred vase-painters were active at any one time.[14] A sizable industry arose to supply the needs of the city, which also required plain black and unglazed serviceable pottery for use as inexpensive table and cooking ware. The output of the finer ware, first in the black-figure and later in the red-figure style, was extensive as it was widely used by all classes, not solely by the wealthiest class. The potters and painters were primarily Athenians handing down their craft from father to son. Undoubtedly, foreign artisans were attracted to this thriving industry in Athens. Foreign-sounding names appear among the vase signatures; among them are Lydos, perhaps the Lydian, and Skythes, possibly the Scythian. The owners of the potteries, usually potters themselves, shared in the general prosperity of the city and some were apparently comfortably affluent. Evidence of this can be found in the existence of various marble dedication inscriptions on the Acropolis, erected by potters. They also placed fine examples of their pottery in sanctuaries and dedicated them to the gods, for a fine terracotta pot was not considered inferior to a bronze one.

An aspect of the industry about which little is known is the marketing and exporting of the pottery. There appears to be some evidence that in addition to selling the ware at the potteries in the Ceramicus, it was also sold in stalls or shops in the Agora and in the streets. Attic pottery has been found at many sites throughout the Mediterranean area and beyond, including France, Germany, Italy, Corsica, Sicily, South Russia, Asia Minor, Mesopotamia, and in the Sudan as far south as Meröe, indicating that its export was an established business. Large numbers of Greek vases have been discovered in Etruscan tombs with Etruscan *graffiti* incised on the under surface of the feet of the vases. The pottery industry in Athens, including manufacturing, financing, trading, and shipping, was of major economic importance to the city.

So rich an industry with so many varied facets deserves a series of detailed studies. Accordingly, this study has been assiduously limited to the chosen topic of the techniques used to produce the painted pottery of Athens.

Chapter One

FORMING THE VASES

3 *Corinthian pinax showing clay being dug, loaded into baskets, and lifted out of a pit.*

CLAY IS AN extremely abundant material which has been formed by the continuous weathering and erosion of the surface of the earth. The outer crust of the earth is composed of many minerals, the most common of which is feldspar, comprising approximately 59% of the total. In the disintegration of feldspar, the alkali part is dissolved and carried away by water. This ultimately leaves alumina and silica which combine with water through hydrolysis to become pure clay. The mineral clay is represented by the formula: $Al_2O_3 \cdot 2SiO_2 \cdot 2H_2O$.

A pure clay which has been formed at the site of the original feldspar, and has not been moved by water, wind, or glacier, is termed a primary or residual clay which is uncontaminated and white. A clay that has been transported from its original location by the forces of erosion is known as a secondary clay, and usually contains mineral or organic impurities acquired in

4 *Modern Attic clay pit near Amarousi, a source used in antiquity and worked into modern times.*

movement or sedimentation. These impurities may affect the color of the fired clay.[1]

Attic clay

Attic clay is a secondary clay in which iron is present as an impurity; this accounts for the rich reddish-brown color. The clay that was used in making Attic pottery was found in various deposits near the city of Athens, one of which adjoins the present-day town of Amarousi.[2] The clay occurs in large surface areas in a relatively pure state, quite simple to mine.[3] This Attic red clay, with its extraordinary working or handling characteristics and handsome color, is one of the finest clays in the world. Its unusual plastic properties allowed the ancient potters of Athens to fashion the most refined shapes on their wheels. Its red color dictated the restrained, sophisticated red and black color combination that was the hallmark of Attic pottery and which was proudly exported to the lands bounding the Mediterranean Sea and beyond.

5 *Modern Attic clay settling basins.*

The ancient clay pits of Amarousi have been worked continously to the present day. Ill. 4 is a photograph taken in 1960 of one of the largest pits. The modern level is about 35 feet below the surface of the surrounding ground. Unfortunately, all traces of the ancient workings have been eradicated owing to the constant digging in the pit. Scattered about are sections of track and dump cars which are used to cart out the clay. This modern clay corresponds in mineral content to the clay used in ancient times, as shown by a comparison of the spectrographic analyses of these clays in column 1 and column 2 in Table I,[4] (see p.198).

Purification of clay

As the clay comes from the pit, it has mixed with sand, small stones, decayed vegetable matter, and other foreign material, all of which has to be removed before the clay can be used. This is accomplished today, as it was in ancient times, by mixing water with the clay and letting the mixture stand in a large settling basin. The heavy impurities fall to the bottom and the upper layer of clay and water is pumped or bailed into an adjoining settling basin. This process is repeated, sometimes several times. Each settling purifies the clay still further until the desired quality is obtained. Obviously a purer clay was required to fashion a delicate kylix than to form a large coarse-bodied storage jar.

5   Ill. 5 shows the settling basins of a modern potter in Amarousi. When the desired purity of the clay is achieved, the water is allowed to evaporate until the clay begins to solidify and to develop drying cracks. The modern potter scores the surface of the hardening clay so that it will crack into blocks of convenient, portable size. These damp clay blocks are stored indoors until needed, and storage of the clay over several months actually helps the working characteristics of the clay. It allows the clay to take a "set" so that, while remaining malleable, the clay will hold its shape during forming on the wheel. The fresh clay often has old clay from a previous batch mixed with it which increases bacterial action and also seems to improve the working of the clay.[5]

Clay deposits are found in many locations in Greece but all clays are not suitable for making pottery; sometimes different clays are blended to vary the color or working properties. This practice was recorded in ancient times in *Geoponica*, VI, 3: "Not all earth is suitable for pottery, but with regard to potter's clay, some prefer the yellowish red, some the white, and others mix the two."[6] A light cream-colored Attic clay was used in the late Helladic and Geometric periods, and then the red clay came into widespread usage.

C. Vassilopoulos & Sons of Athens, manufacturers of modern Greek pottery, generously provided me with samples of three Greek clays: a red Athenian clay from Amarousi; a lighter-colored clay from a deposit on the island of Aegina, near the village of Messagro (not far from the temple of Aphaia); and a brownish clay from Chalkis on Euboea.

Analysis of clay

Spectrographic analyses of these three clays (Table I, columns 2, 3, and 4: see p. 198) show surprising similarities between them. The clay sources are separated by about 100 miles. This shows that clay of high quality was readily available all over Greece; however, the best was found in Athens. Variation in the iron content and the inclusion or absence of decayed vegetable matter probably account for the slight difference in the color of the three clays.

Although the color of the fired modern Attic clay closely resembles that of the fired ancient Attic clay, there are differences in their composition. In Table I, a comparison of column 1 and column 2 shows a greater difference between the ancient and modern Attic clays than between any two of the modern clays tested. These differences in the Attic clays do not affect the production of the black glaze. Obviously, the modern clay comes from a different pit or from a much lower stratum in an ancient pit than does the ancient sample. This merely indicates the extensive working of the Attic clay sources in ancient times.

Shrinkage of clay

The ancient potter had to know the properties of his clay in order to make the best use of it. The shrinkage of clay takes place in two distinct phases. The first phase occurs after the vase is formed, during the thorough drying, but before firing. The second shrinkage happens during the firing process. Measurements show that in Attic clay the linear drying shrinkage is 9%, and the firing shrinkage resulting from a temperature of 945°C. is a $\frac{1}{2}$%, a total of $9\frac{1}{2}$%. This shrinkage is uniform for both vertical and horizontal measurements. The potter had to take this shrinkage into account when he was fashioning the vase. It is most probable that he made the lids for his vases at the same time as he made the vases so that they would both shrink proportionately and still fit after firing.

In the manufacture of large pithoi and terracotta pieces of sculpture, such as statues, antefixes, and other architectural elements, shrinkage was undesirable and temper was therefore added to the clay. This temper consists of sand and sometimes crushed rock. It not only minimizes the shrinkage in drying, but also increases the stiffness and reduces the tendency of the clay to slump during forming. Crushed pottery or grog also could be added to the clay for this purpose, but this was not done in Attic pottery. The presence of temper or grog can be detected easily by examining a fractured edge of a terracotta piece. If either is present the edge will have a coarse texture made up of many very small irregular lumps. This contrasts markedly with the normal Attic pottery which shows a fine-grained homogeneous surface at a fracture.

The shrinkage of Attic clay and the addition of temper to control it is further modified by the firing temperature. Graph I (see p. 200) shows the shrinkage curves for Attic clay, Attic clay with 20% sand temper added by weight, and Attic clay with 40% sand added by weight. The major shrinkage which occurs during drying is reduced from 9% to 6% by the addition of 40% of sand by weight to the clay. This reduces the shrinkage by $33\frac{1}{3}$%. The curves show that at temperatures of over 1000°C. the firing shrinkage becomes substantially increased. Graph III shows that this shrinkage due to vitrification increases the density of the clay body, and correspondingly the hardness, as the firing temperature is increased.

Loss of weight of clay

At the same time that shrinkage occurs, there is a corresponding loss of weight. Graph II shows three curves for the same three test samples. The greatest loss occurs during drying at which time the free water leaves the clay. Attic clay loses 21% of its weight in drying; however, this is reduced to 15% when 40% sand by weight is added to the clay. During the firing, water vapor is driven off, and at the higher temperatures the water molecules which are chemically combined with the clay are lost. When fired at 945°C., Attic clay loses a total of 33% of its weight. The addition of sand substantially reduces this loss, even at higher temperatures, so that at 945°C. the 40% sand and clay mixture loses a total of only 22% of its weight.

Forming techniques

Most Attic black-figured and red-figured vases, with the exception of the so-called plastic vases, were produced on the potter's wheel. This technique, however, was perfected only after a long period of evolution and development. The earliest clay forming technique, invented about 7,000 years ago at the beginning of the Pottery Neolithic period, was the freehand forming of a vessel from a lump of clay. This was accomplished by pushing and pinching the clay until the desired shape was achieved. Examples of this early technique, dating from about 5000 BC, have been found in Jordan, Iran, and Iraq.[7] Even earlier pottery has been reported in the People's Republic of China.

Later this process was improved by the use of strands of clay which were used to build the pot. A thick strand was coiled around a flat hand-formed base disc of clay and then pinched and smoothed to form a good joint. Additional strands were added and consolidated to build the pot to the desired height and shape. To assist in the compacting and smoothing operation, sometimes a rounded stone was held inside against the wall of the pot while the outside surface was beaten with a paddle. Very fine pottery with walls of uniform thickness was produced. This coiled pottery has been compared to the technique of basket weaving in which baskets are woven with long ropes of fiber. It may be that the coiled pottery technique derived from basketry.[8]

A refinement of this technique, which preceded the invention of the potter's wheel, involved forming the pot on a small piece of rush matting or a curved potsherd. The mat or potsherd acted as a base during the building of the pot and as a convenient pivot so that the vessel could be readily rotated between the hands of the potter. This manual rotation gave the potter an opportunity to smooth the pot continually and adjust its symmetry as he built it. Some primitive groups, such as the American Indians, never progressed beyond this technique, and all of their very competent pottery was produced in this way.

The coil method continued to be practiced in Athens, even after the invention of the potter's wheel, in the construction of plain utilitarian pottery intended for daily use. This plain ware, consisting of unglazed cooking pots, water jars, saucers, and common household pottery, was produced at the same time as the more elegant wheel-made pottery.[9] The very large unglazed pithoi, or storage jars, were also made by the coil method.

Potter's wheel

The invention of the potter's wheel occurred near the end of the fourth millennium BC. Its use was not immediately widespread, some areas having adopted it far ahead of others. One of the first areas was in Sumer, about 3250 BC. In Egypt it was used as early as the latter part of the Second Dynasty, about 2750 BC. In Troy, wheel-made pottery was found at the Troy IIb level, about 2500 BC.[10]

Various ancient authors ascribed the invention of the potter's wheel to different sources.[11] However, the earliest Greek reference to the wheel is in Homer, *Iliad*, XVIII, 599–601: "And now they would run around with deft feet exceedingly lightly, as when a potter sitting by his wheel that fitteth between his hands maketh trial of it whether it run."[12]

The Greek wheel was a heavy, sturdily built disc of wood, terracotta, or stone about 2 feet in diameter. On the under side was a socket which fitted over a low fixed pivot. The entire wheel was balanced to run true without wobble or vibration. It was customary practice to have a boy, presumably an apprentice, turn the wheel by hand, adjusting the speed at the command of the potter. Notches around the edge of some wheels afforded a firmer grip. The *1, 6* large size and weight of the wheel provided ample momentum once it was put in motion.[13] Having an assistant for the labor of wheel-turning allowed the potter to use both hands in forming the vase and to devote his entire attention to it. Instead of the potter using his own muscular force to shape the clay, the rotation of the wheel imparted the energy which he directed with his hands. The kick-wheel, or foot-operated wheel, apparently was not used in classical times.

In the early Pottery Neolithic period it is presumed that each family made its own pottery. As most of the household tasks were performed by the women of primitive groups, they probably made the pottery also, while the men were responsible for procuring game and defending the tribe. With the introduction of the potter's wheel and the improved kiln, this work was taken over by a specialist, the professional potter. Undoubtedly, the potter was a man, because the use of a machine was not usually considered women's work. In such a manner the industry evolved in Athens, and the potters congregated in one district of the city called the Ceramicus.

Shapes of vases

All things undergo evolutionary changes and so it was with the design of Attic vases. The tendency from the sixth to the fourth century BC was for the contours to progress from heavy solid shapes to an elegant balance between utilitarianism and beauty, and then to somewhat overly elaborate and attenuated forms. Oddly enough, the emphasis was on perfecting the existing designs rather than on exploring the development of new shapes. There seems to have been little interest in inventing new pottery styles. The constant repetition of standard shapes could have been disastrous; this repetition could have encouraged mass production without any artistic development. However, it was this faithful reiteration of shapes and the striving for perfection within the framework of the shapes that caused Attic pottery to develop in such a magnificent manner. The basic fact that the pottery was intended for daily use gave it a sense of validity and forced it to be practical. This fact prevented the pottery from ever becoming unrealistic and degenerating into merely ostentatious bric-a-brac without regard to function.

The shapes of most Attic vases were based on the cylindrical, conical, or spherical forms which are natural to the wheel. Nearly without exception, the vases are forms in axial balance, symmetrical and poised, held erect by a substantial base, and capped with a mouth and sometimes a lid. The swelling curves, the practical handles, and the ample mouths take advantage of the capabilities, strength, and characteristics of the Attic clay. Its fine-grained texture, cohesion, and working properties are reflected in the shapes that the potters were ultimately able to achieve from it.

The proportions of a vase, the relation of the size of the mouth to the neck, of the neck to the body, and the entire vase to its foot, all fit together as a harmonious whole. Handles appear not as mere appendages added as an afterthought, but as organic parts of the composition of the entire vase. For structural reasons, the handles widen at the point where they join the vase; the

6 Detail of ill. 1; a potter is throwing a vase on the wheel which is being turned by hand by his apprentice.

requirement that they should be strong causes them to emerge gracefully from the vase.

In some Attic vases, the contour is a single unbroken undulating curve. One type of kylix has the lip, bowl, stem, and foot merged in a unified continuous line. Most vases, however, have their sections clearly articulated, and their beauty is based on the harmonious relationships between the various areas. This deliberate articulation allowed the potter to contrast a straight line with a strongly curved one, and a swelling form with an incurving plane. These changes of form also served to mask the points of juncture for the parts of the vase that were thrown separately on the potter's wheel.

The vases were achieved freehand on the wheel with only a pair of dividers and a ruler as a guide. There is no evidence that a template was used either to form the vases or to check the measurements of the subtle, well-proportioned shapes. Efforts have been made to try to show that these proportions were based on carefully worked out geometrical ratios.[14] Ratios do exist, but apparently they were accomplished only by the artistry of the potter's eye and not by numerical formulae.

Fired terracotta is brittle and, in flat strips or in rectangular constructions, does not possess much strength. When shaped in a spherical form, however, fired terracotta is amazingly strong. This is readily accomplished because it is natural to the wheel. The shapes of Attic black-figured and red-figured pottery could be achieved only by the use of the potter's wheel; first, in forming the vase, and second, in refining the shape by the turning or finishing operation.

Forming on the wheel

The production of wheel-made pottery requires a high degree of manual dexterity and a continual application of artistic judgment. The form must evolve slowly, but not too slowly or it will collapse, and it has to be developed to its final state through a series of intermediate steps. The tools of the potter are primarily his nimble fingers aided by a few simple implements. There are no complex tools that can assist him. The only improvement in technique that has been made over the ancient potter is the substitution of an electric motor in place of the boy who turned the wheel. Ironically, the boy probably did a better job, as he had more accurate control of the wheel.

From the study of representations of ancient potters at work, from an examination of Attic pottery itself, and with a knowledge of modern ceramic practice, it is possible to recreate the ancient methods of forming the vases. However, merely to describe in words the wedging, throwing, turning, and joining processes would leave too much to the imagination. Accordingly, a series of photographs, together with brief descriptions, was made to illustrate every step in the making of a Greek vase. It was decided not to pose the photographs, but to take them as the potter worked with the wheel in motion.

For reproduction, an Attic black-figured kylix was chosen, as this delicate shape presents all of the problems of throwing, turning, and joining, and represents the excellence of Attic pottery. Fong Chow, a consummate potter, collaborated with me in analyzing the methods and sequence of production of the ancient counterpart. His hands appear in the series of photographs on 7–64 vase-forming.

7 *The clay is cut in half with a wire.*

8 *The clay is repeatedly wedged by stacking the lower half on the upper.*

9 *Kneading also removes air bubbles.*

10 *When the clay is soft and malleable, it is thrown on the wheel.*

11 *While the wheel revolves, the clay is centered between wet hands.*

12 *When the clay runs true without wobble, a central hole is started.*

13 A heavy wall is formed.

14 The wall is squeezed to broaden and begin to shape the bowl.

15 Outward pressure from inside opens the bowl.

16 Pressure between the fingers shapes the bowl.

17 The bowl is thinned using a wooden shaper.

18 A wet leather strip finishes the lip.

19 *As the wheel revolves, a wire is drawn through the base.*

20 *The bowl is lifted from the wheel.*

21 *The base of the bowl shows the spiral wire marks.*

22 *Clay left on the wheel is used for the foot.*

23 *This clay is centered and drawn up.*

24 *A knob is formed.*

25 *The stem of the foot is smoothed with a metal shaper.*

26 *The foot is flattened.*

27 *A sponge is used to smooth the foot.*

28 *A metal shaper is used to make a shallow hole.*

29 *A wire is slowly drawn through the base.*

30 *The foot is lifted from the wheel.*

31 A hollow support for the foot is modeled.

32 The support is attached to the wheel with clay.

33 As the wheel turns, the support is shaped to run true.

34 When the foot is leather-hard, it is placed in the support.

35 The foot is held in position by soft clay.

36 A metal tool is used to pierce a hole through the foot.

37 *The metal shaper refines the foot during turning.*

38 *When the base of the foot is finished, it is removed.*

39 *Sharp edges and the hole can be seen.*

40 *The foot is centered right side up on the wheel.*

41 *The foot is turned with a metal shaver.*

42 *The foot is refined to its final shape.*

43 *When the bowl is leather-hard, it is centered on the wheel.*

44 *The bowl is held in place with soft clay.*

45 *The bowl is turned with a metal shaver.*

46 *The bowl is thinned and given its correct shape.*

47 *The potter tests its thinness by tapping.*

48 *A wet sponge smoothes the bowl.*

49 *The center is marked for the foot.*

50 *Wet clay is applied as a bond.*

51 *Wet clay is also applied on the foot.*

52 *The foot is positioned.*

53 *Final centering is aligned while the wheel revolves.*

54 *More wet clay is applied around the joint.*

55 *A length of clay is rolled out for the handles.*

56 *The clay is cut to equal lengths.*

57 *The clay is rolled thinner in the middle and tapered.*

58 *The handles are bent to shape.*

59 *The ends are cut at an angle to fit the bowl.*

60 *The cut ends and the bowl are coated with wet clay.*

61 *They are attached to the bowl.*

62 *A wet sponge is used to smooth the joints and surface.*

63 *The forming operation is now completed.*

64 *The kylix is allowed to dry longer before decorating.*

In summary, the process of making a vase starts with wedging or beating the clay to remove air bubbles, to make it homogeneous, and to get the clay to the proper working consistency. A ball of clay is then centered on the rotating wheel and firmly held in cupped hands until it runs true without wobbling. Pressure of the thumb in the center of the ball of clay forms a thick-walled ring which is slowly pulled upward between the thumb and fingers, creating a cylinder. The cylinder then can be either opened into a bowl shape, drawn up as a long tube, flattened into a plate, or closed to form a sphere, at the pleasure of the potter. This process concludes the throwing operation, and the vase is set aside to harden. The following day, when the clay has dried to a firm, leather-hard state, the vase is centered upside down on the wheel. As the wheel rotates, metal, bone, or wood tools are used to "turn" or refine the shape by shaving off unwanted clay. Then a wet sponge is used to smooth the

65 *The inside surface of an amphora showing finger grooves left by the potter.*

66 *Spiral grooves on the base of a votive saucer found in the Athenian Agora, fourth century BC; the grooves were left when the potter removed the saucer from the wheel by means of a cord. Cf. ill. 21.*

vase. The foot of the vase or other sections may be thrown separately, turned, and joined to the body of the vase with clay slip. Finally, the vase, as a combined unit, is turned, and the handles are added. The clay must still be in the somewhat plastic, leather-hard condition when the handles are applied with a clay-slip binder, or they will not adhere. The vase is now finished and ready for decorating and firing.

The marks of the tools used to form the vases were usually eradicated by the potter, but a careful examination will reveal some traces. The inside surface of vases with relatively narrow necks and mouths, such as the amphora, pelike, and hydria, usually show the spiral ridges formed by the potter's fingers as he pulled up the clay during the throwing operation. In 65 vases with large mouths, like the skyphos and krater, these inner surfaces, which would be visible to the user, were carefully smoothed and glazed.

At the completion of the throwing process, the soft clay vase was removed from the wheel by cutting through the base of the vase with a cord or a wire. The wheel was allowed to rotate slowly, while the cord was pulled through the clay. This left the characteristic pattern of spiral grooves on the bottom of 66 the vase.[15] Normally, these grooves were removed in the turning operation which shaped the under-side of the foot, although in the case of very simple pottery these telltale grooves were allowed to remain. Ancient grooves can be compared to the grooves produced while making the copy of a kylix. 21

The bodies of some of the simpler Attic vase shapes, such as the skyphos

35

and pelike, were thrown on the wheel and finished in one piece. Many others, however, like the kylix (chosen for the sequence of illustrations), the lekythos, column krater, and hydria, were thrown in sections which were then joined with a slip of wet clay before being turned and finished on the wheel. The shape in many cases dictated where the joint was to occur; in the kylix it was at the point of juncture between the stem of the foot and the bowl. In a column krater, the joint occurs between the neck and the shoulder. The change of shape at these points tends to hide the joints. However, in large hydriai, or kraters, the body of the vase was so large that it could not be formed properly in one piece, and it was necessary to throw the body in sections. These large bowl and ring sections had to be joined on a continuous curved section where the joint could not be hidden by the articulation. Accordingly, after the sections were thrown and had become firm, they were assembled in their ultimate form and left to harden for a day. The hardening took place in a damp room to prevent too rapid a drying and warpage. Later they were joined with wet clay slip, and the entire section was turned and smoothed so skillfully that on the outside of the vase the joint was not visible. On the inside, however, they can be detected through the variation of 67 thickness, and occasionally, as on the large Apulian volute krater illustrated cf.253 in ill. 67, cracks occur at the junction of the sections.

Forms and uses

Since the shapes of Attic vases reflect their functions, it is easy to determine their use. In addition, drawings on many vases depict scenes in which the uses of vases are clearly portrayed. Also, ancient literary sources not only describe situations in which vases are employed, but in some cases the sources even identify a particular shape by name.

The use of the vase dictated its shape, and the shape indicated the method of construction. It therefore seems appropriate to study the construction of a vase and, at the same time, to examine illustrations of the vase in use. It is not the intention of this work to set forth a comprehensive classification of the shapes of vases, or to try to be definitive about the ancient names that were applied to them. These studies have been undertaken by Gisela M. A. Richter and Marjorie J. Milne in *Shapes and Names of Athenian Vases* (1935). Instead, presented here is a survey of the principal shapes, their construction, and their uses as seen in the drawings on actual vases. All of these vases have slight variations, but a typical style of each shape is illustrated. The vases have been grouped in accordance with the use in which they were most often employed.

67 A crack can be seen on this Apulian volute krater, where two sections were not very skillfully joined.

It is logical that in making a vase the ancient potter tried to form it in the most expeditious manner. Accordingly, he would wish to make the vase in one piece so that later he would not have to join sections, entailing more work and increasing the risk of failure. Small light vases gave him the opportunity to form a vase in one piece, whereas a large vase of the same shape required him to throw it in sections. In the following descriptions of vase shapes, the methods of construction are based on the typical average-size vases. However, all rules have their exceptions. A close examination of a large number of vases most assuredly will reveal deviations from the procedures as described. Although the size of a vase is a determining factor in the method of production, it is quite evident that various potters had their idiosyncrasies. Nevertheless, the steps as described can be accepted as the normal method of making given types of vases.

Amphora

The storage of wine was one of the most common uses for Attic vases. A popular shape for this purpose was the amphora, a vase with two sturdy handles. It was also used to hold olive oil, honey, or water. Amphorae varied widely in size, but there were two predominant types: one with the neck and
68 body forming a continuous curve, and the other with the neck set off from the
69 body by a definite change in contour, called a neck-amphora. The first type is
70 illustrated in use in ill. 70. The body of the vase was thrown in one piece, complete with the mouth ring. When the vase had dried leather-hard it was turned. The foot was thrown separately and joined to the body. The handles, which were formed by rolling two "snakes" of clay in the hands, were added with clay slip.

71   The neck-amphora, as pictured in ill. 71, is a further variation of the type; it lacks a foot and is pointed with a knob finial on the bottom. A ring stand, or tripod, was used to hold this type of amphora upright, or it could have been thrust into a hole in the ground, or leaned in a corner.

In construction, the body of the neck-amphora was usually thrown in one piece including the mouth. The vase was turned and the foot and handles were added later. If a pointed amphora were being made, the slight foot support necessary for throwing the body would be trimmed to a point or a knob in the turning operation.

Amphorae were usually equipped with lids which have been prone to loss or breakage; consequently, not many have been preserved. A lid was thrown at the same time as the amphora so that it could be given a proper fit. It was thrown upside down as a flat flaring dish with a raised flange to fit inside the mouth of the vase. Later its position was reversed and the top surface was turned and smoothed.[16] A knob handle in the form of a pomegranate or pine cone was added which had been thrown separately. During drying, the lid was left on the vase so it would shrink uniformly with the vase. Both the lid and the vase were sometimes marked with the same symbol for identification. Small knobs were thrown solidly but larger ones were made hollow. A tiny hole was made in a hollow knob, sometimes in the top, or in the bottom, or both, to insure proper drying and to prevent breakage during firing from the expanding air within. Some clever potters, however, as a *tour de force*, made the knob with very thin walls and completely closed it, allowing no vent hole. A slow firing was required so that the trapped air could penetrate the thin porous walls and escape without injury to the knob.

A special type of amphora is the panathenaic amphora which was used as a prize in the athletic contests held in Athens every four years. These prize vases

68 Amphora by the Lysippides Painter, the neck and body forming a continuous curve. See ill. 70.

69 Neck-amphora with lid, by Exekias; here there is a definite change in contour between the neck and the body of the vase. See ill. 71.

70 Detail showing a continuous curve amphora, filled with wine, being used by revelers. By the Epeleios Painter.

71 Pointed neck-amphora held by an entertainer.

72,73 *Panathenaic amphora by the Euphiletos Painter, about 520 BC, used as a prize in the athletic contests held in Athens. Athena is depicted on one side; on the reverse is the foot race for which this prize was awarded. Ht 24½ in.*

Panathenaic amphorae

74,75 *(right) Miniature panathenaic amphora, a souvenir or toy prize, fourth century BC. As well as Athena, this vase depicts a race in armor. Ht 3¾ in.*

76,77 *(opposite) Later panathenaic amphorae were taller and had lids. This example, by the Painter of the Kittos Group, was also awarded for a foot race (cf. ill. 73). Ht with lid 34 in. (The olive oil for this vase was collected in 367/366 BC.)*

were extremely large and contained one metretes of olive oil, about 39 liters, made from olives grown on especially designated trees. Scenes on them depict Athena on one side and on the other the event for which the prize was awarded. An inscription on each vase reads: "One of the prizes from Athens." The body, neck, and mouth of these large vases were thrown in one piece. The foot was thrown separately, joined to the vase, and then turned. Stout handles were attached to carry the great weight. The later panathenaic amphorae are taller with larger mouths and lids. In these both the mouth and foot were thrown separately and joined to the body and, of course, the lid and its knob also were thrown separately, joined, and turned. Souvenir or toy prize vases exist; these tiny copies of panathenaic amphorae were thrown in one piece, turned, and the handles added.

72,73

76,77

74,75

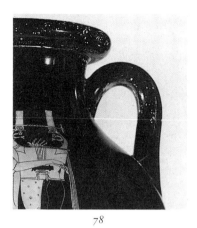

78

79

80

81

82

Handles

78 A single-strand of clay forms the handle of this example by the Berlin Painter.

79,80 Double strand handle on a neck-amphora by the Edinburgh Painter. The two strands of clay can clearly be seen in the side view.

81,82 Triple handle, seen particularly clearly in the side-view, on another neck-amphora.

83,84 A composite, or quadruple handle, on a neck-amphora by the Painter of Group E.

83

84

85   86   87

85 This example by the Lykaon Painter shows a twisted strand handle, made by twining strands together.

86,87 A modified cylindrical handle with a central ridge, by the Achilles Painter.

88,89 A flat strap handle, made by beating a ball of clay into a flat sheet and cutting out the required section. This example is by the class of Cabinet des Médailles 218.

90,91 A flanged handle, made from three flat strips joined with wet clay slip, is shown on this amphora which recalls the Rycroft Painter.

88   89

90   91

Handles

Handles are both a functional and a decorative feature of Greek vases; their many forms and techniques of manufacture are best displayed in the varieties employed on amphorae. Modern potters make handles by pulling them from a thick, wet strand of clay, and repeatedly drawing the clay through their hands like milking a cow. With each stroke the clay becomes more elongated, thinner and tapered, until the desired size and shape is obtained. Other modern handles are made by pressing clay in plaster molds. The ancient Attic potters did not use these methods but rolled lumps of clay between their hands or on a flat surface until they formed long ropes or "snakes" of clay. These "snakes" were modified or combined at the potter's discretion.

78–85   The single-strand handle, cylindrical in cross-section, was the most common. Double, triple, and quadruple or composite handles were also employed. Usually, the quadruple strands were set on top of a flat strap-like handle to gain added support. Sometimes flat handles were grooved with tools to resemble composite ones. Twisted handles, an attractive variation, were made by twining together three, four, or more strands.

86–91   A cylindrical handle could be modified to have a central ridge by smoothing on a thin roll of clay, or by tooling. Flat strap handles were made by beating a ball of clay into a flat sheet and cutting out the required sections. The flanged handle was made from three flat strips joined with wet clay slip.

Pelike

The pelike was also used for the storage of wine and is, in fact, a variety of
92 amphora. It is a squat vase with the greatest width of the body concentrated in the lower half. Undoubtedly, the pelike was a useful and substantial shape,
93 because it tended to resist being tipped. The body and mouth were made in one operation; after turning, the vase was completed by adding the foot and two handles.

Pithos

For the storage of large quantities of wine, water, or grain, a big storage jar, or pithos, was used. Pithoi often were so large that they were sunk into the
94 ground except for the upper part and mouth. This made access to the contents easier, and protected and reinforced the vase. Most pithoi were covered with lids to preserve the contents from evaporation or contamination. In the vase drawing illustrated, Herakles lifts the large stone serving as a lid and the

92 *A variety of amphora known as a pelike, by Polygnotos.*

93 *This example, in the manner of the Altamura Painter, shows a pelike on the floor between two figures. Its substantial shape helped to avoid tipping.*

94 *This detail by a painter near the Acheloos Painter shows Herakles and a centaur taking the lid off a large pithos buried in the ground up to its neck.*

centaur, Pholos, starts to dip his two-handled drinking cup, a kantharos, into the wine.

Small pithoi were thrown in one piece, or in several sections, on the potter's wheel and then joined while damp. Larger pithoi were built by the coil method, probably in a series of steps, allowing the clay to become firm before more clay was added to increase the height. This has been described in *Geoponica*: VI, 3: "Potters do not use the wheel for all pithoi, but only for the small ones. The larger ones they build up day by day, placing them on the ground in a warm room, and thus make them large."[17]

A similar operation by modern local potters on Crete was observed by Roland Hampe and Adam Winter.[18] While working continuously over a period of fifteen hours, the Cretan potters constructed a series of ten pithoi, each about 40 inches in height and 32 inches in diameter. They set up a row of ten flat wheels on which were placed hand-formed clay pithoi bases. Large ropes of clay were kneaded by hand along the rim of each flat clay base following the coil pottery method. The wheels were not true potter's wheels; they were turntables that were turned very slowly, and only from time to time, to aid in making the vases symmetrical. Each vase was allowed to stand and harden after a complete ring of clay had been attached and shaped by hand. A pithos was built in six steps, and the walls on the inside were reinforced where the joints were made. The vases, when dry, were so heavy that two men were required to carry each pot to the kiln.

Some ancient pithoi were so large that they were constructed over collapsible wooden cores which were removed before the clay dried. Pollux, *Onomasticon*, VII, 164: "That around which those who make pithoi put the clay and shape it – this wooden core is called κάναβος."[19] Such pithoi were large enough to hold a man easily. The largest pithoi were fired right where they were made, as the great weight of the dried clay would cause them to break if an attempt was made to move them. A crude kiln or open fire could have been built over the pithos. Since they were not glazed, a simple oxidizing firing was sufficient.

The difficulty of constructing such huge vessels was well appreciated in ancient times. A popular axiom admonished the overly ambitious but inexperienced person from undertaking a project beyond his abilities. He was reminded that a potter learns his craft by first making small vases before he attempts to construct a pithos. *Corpus Paroemiographorum Graecorum*. Zenobius, III, 65: " 'I learn the potter's craft on the pithos'; a proverb upon those who skip the first lessons, and immediately attempt greater things; as if anyone who was learning to be a potter, before learning to mold plates or any other small thing, should undertake a pithos."[20]

95 Women filling hydriai with water at a fountain house; by the A. D. Painter.

Hydria

For the fetching and storage of water a hydria was used, a large pitcher-shaped vase with three handles. Two small horizontal side handles were used 95 to lift the hydria and the third and larger vertical one at the back of the vase was held while pouring. Water was obtained at the local fountain house by the women who congregated every morning and evening to fill their hydriai and exchange gossip. When they carried the empty hydriai they balanced the vases on their heads in a horizontal position. When the hydriai were filled the women lifted them to their heads by the two small side handles and, balancing them erect on a small head pad, they carried them home.

There are two types of hydriai, one in which the neck is set off from the 96,97 shoulder and the shoulder from the body, and the other, called a kalpis, in 98,99 which the neck, shoulder, and body form a continuous curve. In the articulated hydria the body, including the shoulder, was thrown first. The mouth and neck were thrown as one separate piece and to specific measurement in order to fit properly with the body. The foot was also thrown as a separate piece. After drying to a leather-hard state, they were all joined and turned. Lastly, the three handles were attached.

In the case of a very large hydria, the body was thrown in two sections joined about half way up the body wall. The upper part of the body, including the shoulder, was thrown upside down with the same diameter as the lower half. Most likely a large wooden compass was used as a caliper for measurement.

The kalpis was thrown with the body, neck, and mouth as one piece. Only the foot was thrown separately and later attached. The three handles were applied after the vase was turned.

The remarkable handling qualities of Attic clay permitted the making of vases of very complicated shapes, and the kalpis, with its curved shoulder, was particularly difficult. In throwing the top of the shoulder of the vase in a horizontal plane, only the skill of the potter and the cohesion of the clay kept *100* the vase from collapsing. In forming the Campanian hydria shown in ill. 100, an accident occurred and the shoulder partially collapsed, throwing the neck out of plumb.

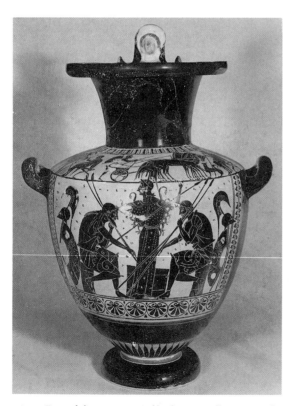

96,97 One of the two types of hydriai (see ills. 98,99), this example attributed to the Leagros Group: the neck is set off from the shoulder, and the shoulder from the body.

98,99 (above) The second type of hydriai (see ills. 96,97), the kalpis, in which the neck, shoulder, and body form a continuous curve. By the Troilos Painter.

100 Campanian hydria with a partially collapsed shoulder.

Krater

The Greeks rarely drank their wine undiluted; usually it was mixed with water. The dilution varied from a one-to-one mixture to one part wine and ten parts water. The importance of the occasion and the wealth of the host indicated the proportions; the guest of honor was often asked to name the *101* ratio. The wine and water were poured into a large mixing bowl, a krater. There are four types of kraters: column, volute, calyx, and bell, identified by their contour and the positions of their handles. They all have in common a large mouth to allow for ladling out the wine mixture.

In throwing the column krater, the body and shoulder were usually formed in one piece. In very large vases of any shape, the weight of the clay forced the potter to throw the body in two sections to be joined later, as previously discussed. The neck and flat lip were thrown together upside down on the wheel as a large ring, the foot was thrown separately, and the three pieces were assembled and turned. Two extensions of the lip were modeled freehand and added on opposite sides. Lastly, the four rod supports for these extensions, the columnar handles, were added. They gave additional strength *102* to the lip for lifting.

The volute krater is identified by its handles curving upwards and ending in *103* large volutes above the lip. The body and shoulder were thrown in one piece, the neck and lip as a separate piece, and the foot also separately. These three elements were assembled and then turned. The spirals of the two volute handles were assembled by joining clay discs to flat strips of clay to form two closed drums. The lower parts of the handles were also made freehand and applied with the two drums. In Attic volute kraters a section of the drum is cut

101 Detail showing a krater, containing wine and water, being used by revelers. By the Epeleios Painter.

102 Column krater, by Myson.

103 Volute krater, so-named because its decorative handles curve upwards and end in large volutes above the lip. By the Painter of Woolly Satyrs. Cf. pl. VII.

104 (below, left) Calyx krater, in the manner of Polygnotos; the body resembles the calyx of a flower.

105 (below, right) Bell krater, by the Persephone Painter, shaped like an inverted bell.

away between the lip of the vase and the lower part of the handle. This arrangement concealed the holes which were needed to allow the drums to dry properly without cracking and to prevent bursting in the firing. In South Italian volute kraters, the technique is usually modified by piercing a round hole in the top of the drums rather than underneath.

104   The body of the calyx krater is in the shape of the calyx of a flower. The two handles are set low on either side of the body. In throwing, the body and lip were made as one piece and the foot thrown separately. After joining and turning, the two handles were added.

105   The bell krater takes its name from its inverted bell-like shape. The body and mouth were thrown as a single piece, and the foot thrown separately. They were joined, turned, and the two small horizontal handles were added high on the body near the lip.

Stamnos

106 The stamnos was still another vase used to hold wine or water. The body, shoulder, neck, and lip, were thrown as one piece, and the foot thrown

107 separately. Its two small handles were added high on the body after turning. The lid for the stamnos was thrown, as was the knob. They were joined and turned.

106 Wine being ladled from a stamnos; detail of a stamnos assigned to the Kensington Class.

107 Stamnos attributed to the Deepdene Painter.

108 Lebes, a vase thrown completely in one piece.

Lebes

The lebes or dinos, a wine mixing bowl, is a large rounded vessel with no foot   *108, 109*
or handles, and was made to be supported on a stand. It is one of the very few
Attic vase shapes thrown completely in one piece; consequently no joining
was required, only the turning operation.

109 Lebes on a stand being filled with wine; detail of a stamnos by Smikros.

Psykter

The Athenians preferred to drink their wine after it had been cooled. Chilled wine was achieved with the use of a wine cooler, or psykter, a bulbous vase *III* with a deep hollow stem. The psykter was almost completely filled with wine and floated in a large krater of cold water, or stuck in snow or ice. When the *IIo* wine had cooled, it was ladled from the psykter.[21] The psykter was thrown as a single piece and required no joining, only turning. Some psykters had small loop or tube handles, added high on the shoulder, through which a cord was passed. The cord served as a handle to help lift the psykter from the krater of cold water. Only the psykters with handles had lids, the others did not. The lids were thrown in two pieces, the lid and the knob, then joined and turned.

Oinochoe

II2 Wine was often ladled from a krater by means of a small pitcher, an oinochoe. There are many variations of the shapes of oinochoai. However, from the standpoint of construction, there are two basic types: first, a continuous *II3* curve from the base of the body to the lip of the mouth; second, a strong point *II4* of articulation between the shoulder and the neck. Either type of oinochoe

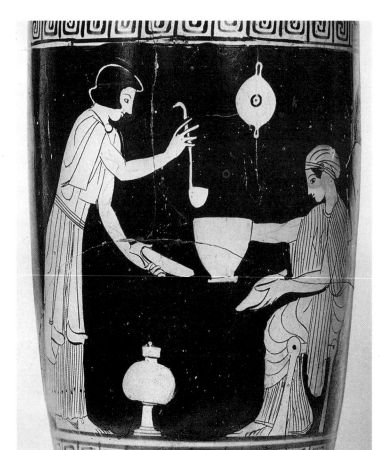

110 A psykter, or wine cooler, with lid, can be seen on the floor between the two figures. By the Pan Painter.

111 Psykter, a distinctive bulbous vase for cooling wine.

may have a plain or a trefoil-shaped mouth. The continuous-curve oinochoe was thrown as a single piece and, after turning, a handle was added. The chous and the olpe are variations of this type. The body of the articulated oinochoe was thrown together with the foot. The mouth and neck were thrown as a separate piece; it was then joined with the body, turned, and the handle added. If a trefoil mouth was desired for either type of oinochoe, it was made immediately after throwing, while the clay was still soft. Two sides of the mouth were pressed in, and the three pouring lips were pulled out. This was done so the server could pour the wine either forward or to the left or right.

Kyathos

A different type of wine ladle was the kyathos, a thin-bodied cup with a high *115* delicate handle. The terracotta kyathos is a pottery adaptation of a metal ladle. Its handle is high, so that the hand would not touch the liquid. The bowl and foot were thrown together and turned, and the handle was formed freehand before it was attached to the bowl. The tiny finial was shaped by rolling it in the fingers, and then attached.

112 Wine being ladled from a krater by means of an oinochoe. By the Dokimasia Painter.

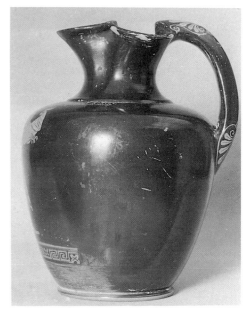

Wine ladles

113 (above) Oinochoe, by the Berlin Painter. This type is shaped in one continuous curve.

114 (right, above) Oinochoe, by the Pan Painter. This type makes a clear distinction between the shoulder and the neck.

115 (right) Kyathos, a delicate cup with a large handle.

Kylix

Drinking cups constitute a large category, because the Athenians drank the mixture of wine and water from many different types of vessels. The most graceful and popular cup was the kylix, which has a wide shallow bowl *116* balanced on a stemmed foot. The handles of the kylix served for carrying and permitted it to be hung on a peg in the wall. The handles also were employed in playing the game *kottabos* as the banqueter is doing in ill. 117 with *117* one of his kylikes. A finger was crooked through a handle and then, with a snap of the wrist, the dregs of wine remaining in the kylix were flipped at a target across the room. If the aim of the reveler was accurate, he dislodged a flat metal disc at the top of a metal stand which then fell with a loud satisfying clang.

The three main types of kylikes are shown in ills 118–120. In the first type, *118–120* the lip is set off from the body; in the second, the bowl is deep and full; and in the third, there is an almost unbroken continuous curved line from the edge of the lip to the bottom of the foot. This last style, with its large gently curving shallow bowl and elegant silhouette, is a triumph of the potter's art. All of these kylikes were made in the same manner as described in detail in ills 7–64. *7–64* Basically, the bowl and foot were thrown as two separate pieces which were then turned and joined. Even the largest bowls were thrown as a single piece. They required a very large base support during throwing which was removed in turning. The foot was thrown upside down for greater control. Two handles were rolled out freehand and added to the vase.

Occasionally, when the foot of a kylix was being joined to the bowl, *51* unfired black glaze matter was used as a binder rather than the customary wet clay slip. The black glaze matter is quite sticky and would work very well. It has been noted that the foot of a kylix usually is not flat but curves up slightly. This was not deliberate, but resulted from warpage in drying due to the thin outer edge and a thicker center section.

Kantharos

Another drinking cup was the kantharos, a rare type of vase with two large *121* upright handles and a deep bowl usually set on a stemmed foot. Dionysus is *122* often shown holding one. Perhaps a kantharos was not a real drinking cup, but was intended for use in tombs and sanctuaries. It was made in the same manner as a kylix; the bowl and foot were thrown separately, then turned and joined, and handles were added last. In the stemless kantharos, the foot was thrown with the body.

Drinking cups

116 (above, left) A reveler balancing a kylix full of wine. By the Villa Giulia Painter.

117 (above, right) A banqueter playing kottabos with kylikes. Detail of a kylix near the Kleophrades Painter.

118 Offset lip kylix, by the potter Tleson, son of Nearchos.

119 Deep bowl kylix, by the Painter of Louvre F 28.

120 Continuous curve kylix, by the Painter of Bologna 417.

121 *Kantharos, by the Nikosthenes Painter, signed by the potter Nikosthenes.*

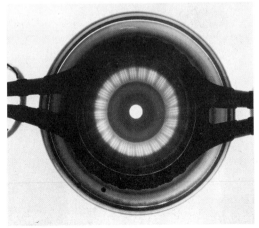

122 *(left) Dionysus pouring a libation from a kantharos.*

123 *(above) X-ray of a black glazed and gilded kantharos, fourth century* BC. *This is a trick vase with two clay pellets in the hollow rim that could be rattled when the cup was empty. See pl. VI.*

Skyphos

The skyphos, or kotyle, also a wine cup, is a deep two-handled cup which does not have a stem and has only a slight foot or ring base. The skyphos is not a particularly handsome vase shape, being fairly squat, but it held a copious amount of wine and was a very serviceable cup. It was thrown and turned as a single piece with only the handles attached later. In the case of a very large skyphos the foot was thrown separately.

Rhyton

The rhyton is a horn-shaped drinking cup that apparently was made in imitation of archaic drinking vessels of real horn. Sometimes animal heads were added to the lower smaller end of the rhyton and, occasionally, a hole was pierced through the bottom. Such a hole had to be held closed by a finger when wine was in the rhyton. For drinking, the vase was held over the head and the finger released to allow the wine to flow into the mouth, or, to aerate the wine, into a cup. Rhyta were made in part using molds; the process is described in detail at the end of this chapter. The molded section, often an animal head, was kept in a partially damp state while the mouth was thrown and turned on the wheel. Then the two sections were joined with wet clay slip and the line of juncture was carefully smoothed to make it invisible. The handle was attached to both the wheel-formed mouth and to the molded head. Sometimes a wheel-formed foot was used as a support.[22]

60

125 *Skyphos, by the Lewis Painter (Polygnotos II).*

126 *Reveler aerating wine from a rhyton. By the Painter of the Philocleon Reverse-Group.*

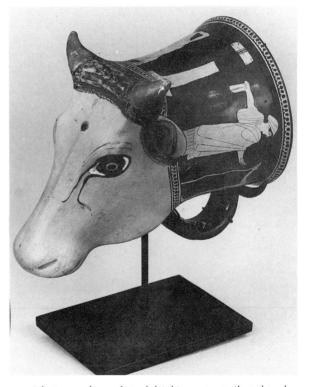

127 *Rhyton, or horn-shaped drinking cup, attributed to the Cow-head Group.*

128 *Woman pouring a libation of wine into a phiale. By the Altamura Painter.*

129 *Phiale, by the Painter of the Boston Phiale.*

130 Flat plates too were thrown on the wheel.

Phiale

A very simple vase form is the phiale, a shallow bowl without handles and often with a central boss that protruded up into the center of the bowl. It was used to pour a libation. Customarily the wine was poured from an oinochoe into a phiale. Then the phiale was slowly tipped, to allow the wine to flow onto the ground or onto an altar fire as an offering. The phiale was thrown and turned as one piece. The central boss, which was useful in holding the phiale from underneath for pouring a libation, was left as a mound in throwing. In turning, the vase was centered upside down and the boss was hollowed out.

129

128

Plate

Even flat plates used for olives, fruit, or meat, were thrown on the wheel. Undoubtedly, the potter centered a large lump of clay and proceeded to form one plate after another, cutting them off with his cord, probably without stopping the wheel. The under-sides were turned later.

130

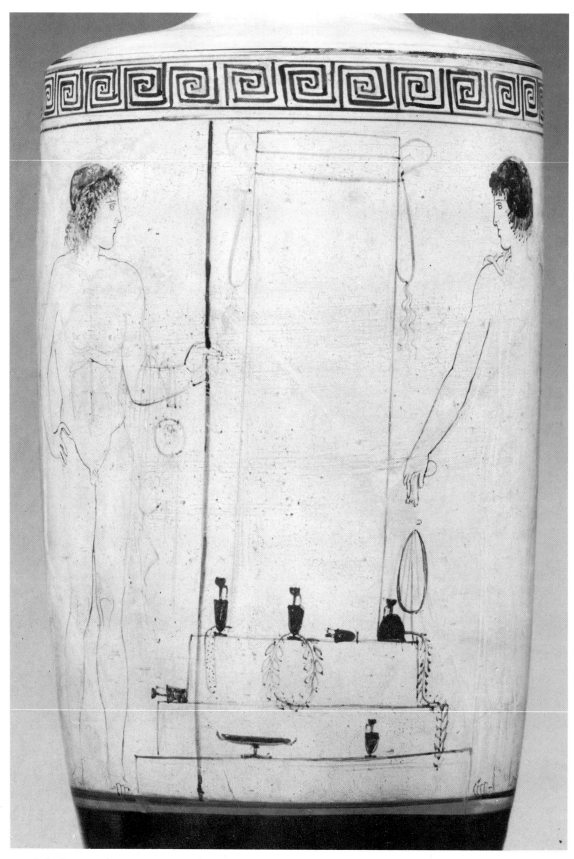

131 *Lekythoi were the most common oil containers. Many of the smaller lekythoi, containing perfumed olive oil, were placed on graves. By the Bosanquet Painter.*

132 Lekythos of olive oil held by a woman at a tomb, by the Inscription Painter. See ill. 136.

Lekythos

Almost all Attic vases were made to hold one of three different liquids, all essential to the Greek way of life: wine, water, and olive oil. The individual shapes were designed for ease of handling, convenience, and practicability, but always with an eye for beauty. Nowhere is this better shown than in the special vases for holding the valuable heavy fluid, olive oil.

Athena is credited with having given Athens the gift of the original olive tree from which sprang all olive trees. Not only was the fruit of the trees eaten, but also a great quantity of oil was used in cooking, as a food, as a body oil, fuel for lamps, as a perfume base, and as an offering for the dead. The oil was stored in large amphorae and later transferred to smaller vases adapted for each particular use. The lekythos, a tall cylindrical vase with a narrow neck, a cup-shaped mouth, and a single handle, was the most common oil container. *132* The narrow neck allowed the oil to be poured in a fine stream, or in drops; the mouth was constructed with a sharp edge on the inside to cut off the flow of oil without dripping.

133 Lekythos, by the Pharos Painter, shaped in one continuous curve.

134 Lekythos with distinct shoulder, by the Tithonos Painter.

There are three shapes of lekythoi. They are given here in their chronological order: one with a continuous curve from the neck to the base, one with the shoulder set off from the body, and the squat lekythos with a broad body and a curving shoulder. The first type was thrown and turned in one piece and only the handle was added. In the second type, the body and foot were thrown together, the shoulder and neck as a separate piece, and the mouth also as a separate piece. All three sections were turned individually, then joined and turned together. The handle was added last. The squat lekythos was thrown as a single piece except for the mouth, which was thrown separately. Both units were turned and joined; then the handle was added.

Many of the smaller lekythoi, containing perfumed olive oil, were placed on graves. Larger lekythoi, often made as tomb offerings, are the white-ground lekythoi, so called because there is a coating of white clay slip over the red Attic clay. Ingenious potting is evident in one particular type of large white-ground lekythoi which were usually thrown in three main sections: the

133–135

131

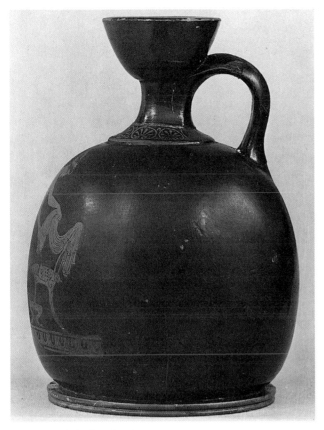

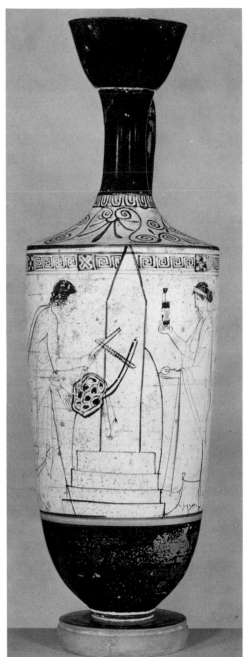

135 Squat lekythos, by the Eretria Painter.

136–138 White-ground lekythos by
the Inscription Painter (above right).
The x-ray of this vase (right) shows
the inner container for oil, and the
detail (below right) shows the vent
hole between the handle and neck
which prevented the vase bursting
during firing.

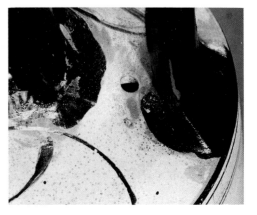

mouth, the neck and shoulder, and the body and foot. The amount of perfumed oil required to fill such a vase was considerable, in some cases a quart or two. Apparently, to certain thrifty Athenians this was an unnecessary waste of expensive oil, or perhaps there was a decree forbidding *136* the waste of oil,[23] and a modification of the lekythos was designed.[24] This modification consisted of forming a small cup, capable of holding only a few ounces, which was inserted inside the vase, attached to the lower part of the neck. This false bottom was hidden when the component parts of the vase were assembled and fired, and the finished vase, to all intents, appeared to hold a full quantity of oil. In intact vases, these inner cups can be seen in x-ray *137* photographs. The cup sealed the bottom of the neck and thus created an airtight space in the balance of the base. During firing, the expansion of the air in the sealed part of the vase could cause it to burst, so a small vent hole was provided. At first, the hole was placed on the shoulder, later under the foot, and in still later modifications the hole was inconspicuous on the shoulder *138* between the handle and the neck, but it sometimes was placed low on the body. C. H. E. Haspels gives credit to the Beldam Potter for being the first to make false-bottomed tomb-lekythoi.[25]

The shapes of the inner container have been studied by Dietrich von Bothmer who has observed that different shapes occur in the lekythoi of different vase-painters. For example, in the lekythoi of the Villa Giulia Painter they are cone shaped; cylindrical in shape in the vases of the Sabouroff Painter; and globular or bag shaped in the lekythoi of the Achilles Painter.

After the vase was assembled, and before decorating, a thin coating of white clay slip was applied over the body and shoulder; this was done on the rotating potter's wheel to obtain a very even layer of the white clay.

Aryballos

Athletes carried a small container, an aryballos, filled with oil to anoint their bodies as a lubricant and to cleanse the skin after exercising. This small vase had one or two miniature handles for attaching a thong to loop over the wrist *141* or to hang on the wall. Aryballoi are usually globular in shape with either a *139,140* broad flat mouth, or a hemispherical mouth. The shape of the mouth permitted the vase to be inverted on the body of the athlete, and facilitated spreading the oil. The method of construction is the same for both types. The body was thrown and turned as a single piece and the mouth was separately thrown and turned. After the two elements were joined, the handles were added. Occasionally, the bottom was formed flat so that the aryballos could be set down without turning over.

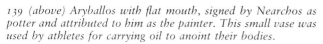

139 (above) Aryballos with flat mouth, signed by Nearchos as potter and attributed to him as the painter. This small vase was used by athletes for carrying oil to anoint their bodies.

140 (above, right) Aryballos with hemispherical mouth.

141 (right) Youth pouring olive oil from an aryballos. By Euphronios.

142 (below) Alabastron, by the Persephone Painter, used for dispensing scented oils.

143 (below, right) Woman holding an alabastron containing scented oil. By the Achilles Painter.

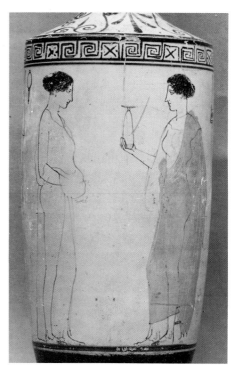

Alabastron

Scented oils, widely used by women, were dispensed from an alabastron or
143 perfume flask. The flask had an elongated body, round on the bottom, with a
142 narrow neck for limiting the flow of the expensive oils. The Attic alabastron
copied its shape from a similar Egyptian vase which was turned from
alabaster. The Attic vase was thrown as a complete piece including its flat
mouth. In turning, the bottom was rounded; later, two lugs were added high
on the body. They were used to attach a cord for suspension.

Plemochoe

144 A larger container for perfume was the plemochoe, or kothon, a covered bowl
with an incurving rim, a stem, and a sturdy foot. The construction of the
turned-in rim and fitted lid made the plemochoe useful for carrying perfume
145 without spilling. The bowl was thrown as a single piece, including the rim.
The potter first threw a spherical shape and then turned the rim in and down.
While the wheel continued to spin, he pressed down on the sphere and
partially flattened it. The turned-in rim is not unlike the turned-down rim on
the outside of a South Italian Apulian fish plate. The stem and foot were
thrown separately, joined to the bowl, and both were turned together. The lid
of the plemochoe, or kothon, was thrown separately and fitted to measure.
Small knobs were thrown as part of the lid and large ones thrown separately
and joined.

Pyxis

Another vase used by women was the pyxis, a cosmetic box to contain rouge
and other toilet articles.[26] Several shapes were popular, all of them rather
148 small and fitted with covers. Knobs were on some of the lids, and a few had
146 bronze rings, some of which have remained intact until the present day. A
147 pyxis was thrown as a simple low cylinder and turned as a single piece.
Notches were sometimes cut into a ring foot to create individual feet. The lid
and knob, if any, were thrown and turned separately.

Lekanis

A lekanis, also used by women, was a flat covered bowl with a low foot and
149 two handles. The lid usually had a large flat knob. It was considered a proper
150 wedding gift and was used to hold trinkets, cosmetics, and hot dishes. The

144 *The plemochoe, another perfume container.*

145 *Woman with a plemochoe containing perfume. By the Eretria Painter.*

146 *Pyxis, or cosmetic box, with knob on the lid. By the Penthesilea Painter.*

148 *Pyxis carried by a woman. By the Marsyas Painter.*

147 *Pyxis with a ring on the lid.*

149 Lekanis, lidded bowl used by women.

150 (below) Girl offering a lekanis to a seated bride. By the Marsyas Painter.

151 Lebes gamikos, or ceremonial water bowl used by a bride. By the Washing Painter. See ill. 153.

152 (left) Lebes gamikoi being used in a home. By the Eretria Painter.

body and foot were thrown together and turned. The lid was thrown upside down, as all lids were, and the knob, if large, was thrown separately and attached. The two horizontal side handles were attached last.

Lebes gamikos

At the time of a wedding a lebes gamikos, or marriage bowl, a special type of lebes, was placed in the home of a bride. This was a ceremonial water bowl *152* rather than a functional container. There were two types, one with a high conical stand joined to the bowl, and the other with a simple ring base. Both had large vertical double loop handles and a conical lid with a pomegranate *151* knob finial. The body was thrown as a bowl, complete with neck and lip. The conical stand was thrown separately upside down. The lid was also thrown upside down and the knob finial was thrown separately, and joined and turned later. The lebes and the stand were turned separately, then joined and turned together. The double loop handles were added last. If the conical stand was not used, the ring base was thrown as part of the bowl and was finished in turning.

Loutrophoros

The symbolic bridal bath, a different wedding custom, was given to the bride in water from a loutrophoros hydria. This was a special type of hydria, very *153* much elongated with a high foot, tall neck, and large mouth. The three handles were also elongated; two small vertical loop handles at the sides, and the large vertical handle at the rear, extended to reach the mouth. The body *155* was thrown as one section, and the mouth, neck, and foot were also thrown separately. The vase was assembled, joined, and turned, after which the handles were added.

Another special vase was made for funeral purposes. A loutrophoros amphora was sometimes placed at the grave of those who died unwed. In the vase drawing, one is being held by mourning women. This type of amphora *154* has an elongated body and neck with a wide mouth and two large vertical engaged handles. Usually the bottom of the vase was left open so that libations poured into the vase at the grave would flow directly into the ground. The vase was thrown in three sections: the body, the neck and mouth, *156* and the foot. The parts were assembled and turned. Flat strips of clay were used to form the two large handles and the engaging struts.

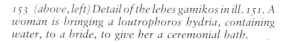

153 (above, left) Detail of the lebes gamikos in ill. 151. A woman is bringing a loutrophoros hydria, containing water, to a bride, to give her a ceremonial bath.

154 (above) Loutrophoros amphora held by a woman in mourning. See ill. 156.

155 (left) Loutrophoros hydria, by the Painter of Louvre MN 558.

156 (below) Loutrophoros amphora from which the detail in ill. 154 was taken.

Miscellaneous

The foregoing covers the most important wheel-made pottery. There are minor types, such as saucers, beakers, mugs, stands, funnels, lamps, and lamp fillers. The construction of these minor types was simple and is self-evident; therefore, we will not examine them in detail. The basic processes of throwing pieces on the wheel, and later turning and refining them, are applicable.

Mold-made pottery

The other type of Attic pottery made during the black-figure and red-figure period was the so-called plastic vases which were partially formed in molds. The output of ancient mold-made pottery is slight compared with the quantity produced on the wheel. In modern ceramic practice, mold-made pottery is the most common type, but it is manufactured by a different process, a casting process. For comparative purposes the casting process is described here, although it was never used for ancient Attic pottery. A liquid clay slip, called a casting slip, is poured into a plaster mold. It is allowed to remain until the plaster absorbs the moisture of the clay slip near the surface of the mold, causing this layer to solidify. This takes about an hour. The mold is then inverted and the remaining slip is poured out. After the thin-walled clay casting has hardened slightly, the mold is carefully opened and the casting removed. The hollow clay casting is retouched, finished by hand, and subsequently fired.

The manufacturing procedure of ancient mold-made ware began with the forming of the original model. The patrix, or master model, was made from clay by a sculptor, keeping in mind the ultimate use of the vase and the intermediate manufacturing steps. In most plastic vases, the mold-made section was joined to a part, usually the mouth, and sometimes a foot, formed on the potter's wheel. Therefore, the patrix was made for only the molded section. An excellent example of a patrix is that of a deer head in The Metropolitan Museum of Art reported to have come from Taranto in Apulia. *157* Much work has been done on this subject by Herbert Hoffmann, who first recognized and published this unique piece.[27]

This terracotta patrix was designed for the production of a deer-head rhyton, or drinking cup. It was vigorously modeled and left unfinished at the neck where a wheel-formed mouth would be added to the vase. The antlers and ears, which were not suitable for forming in a mold, were omitted; their locations were indicated with small lumps of clay. After the patrix had dried

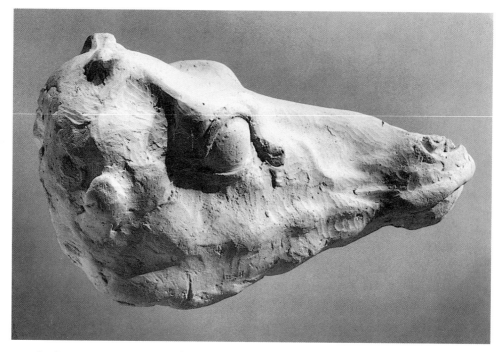

157 Apulian patrix, or master model, for a deer-head rhyton, or drinking-cup. Ht 2¾ in.

and had been fired it was ready to be used in the production of a mold. The patrix was cleverly designed to eliminate undercutting, which would be very difficult to reproduce with a mold.

The deer-head patrix was intended to form a two-piece mold which would separate on a line, bisecting the head in two equal parts, running between the antler stumps, eyes, nostrils, and under-side of the jaw. The mold was made by carefully covering only one side of the patrix with clay, then coating the edge of clay which bisected the head with a substance that was probably animal fat or potash. This substance insured a ready cleavage from the clay which was next coated over the other side of the patrix. When the two halves of the mold had dried slightly and had become firm, they were removed from the patrix and allowed to dry completely. The mold was retouched by hand and fired.

A different method of creating the line of separation in the mold, which may have been employed, utilized a piece of string. It would have been laid on the surface of the patrix following the intended line of separation. The entire patrix and string would then have been covered with clay, and later the string would have been pulled up through the clay, cutting it into the two sections.

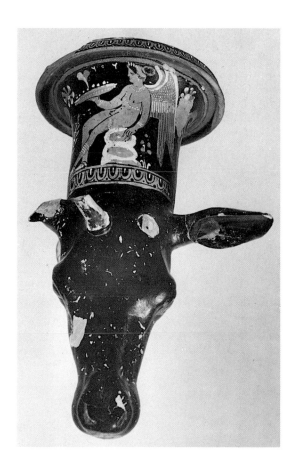

Mold-made pottery

158 (above) Apulian deer-head rhyton, not made from the patrix in ill. 157, but similar. Ht 8¼ in. See Chapter 1, note 27; cf. ill. 127.

159 (above, right) Janiform kantharos, with the head of a satyr and a woman conjoined. The mouth was made on the wheel and joined to the mold-made parts.

160 (right) Askoi, used for filling lamps with oil, in the form of lobster claws. Both are 6¼ in. long and have been assigned to the Class of the Seven Lobster-Claws by J. D. Beazley.

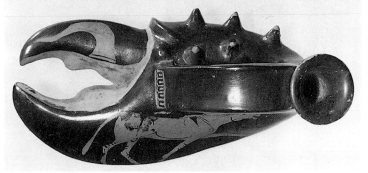

The patrix was made of terracotta rather than wax or some other perishable substance, because a permanent type of patrix would allow an unlimited number of molds to be made from it.

A layer of soft clay was pressed into each of the two sections of the fired terracotta mold. Then the edges of the clay were scored and coated with clay slip for better adhesion, and the two halves of the mold were placed together and bound in position. Additional soft clay was smeared over the joint on the inside of the mold. Within a few hours, the clay would have dried slightly and shrunk away from the surface of the mold. The mold was then opened and the piece removed. In the case of the deer-head rhyton, a mouth section was thrown on the wheel and attached to the molded head with clay slip. A handle was formed freehand and attached in the same manner. Lastly the antlers and ears were modeled and attached at the indicated locations. After drying, the rhyton was ready for decorating and firing. A similar deer-head rhyton, also said to be from Taranto, but not made from the same patrix, is illustrated in
158 ill. 158.[28]

This same mold technique was used to make rather limited quantities of other plastic vases in the shape of human figures and heads. Typical of this type of production is a kantharos with the head of a satyr and a woman
159 conjoined. The mouth was made on the wheel and joined to the mold-made parts.

Two vases made from the same mold and patrix are a pair of Attic plastic
160 askoi which were used for filling lamps with oil.[29] They are in the form of a lobster claw with a wheel-made mouth. The handles and the projections on the side of the claws were molded freehand. The walls of these askoi are very thin, and this was accomplished by very carefully pressing a thin layer of clay in the mold. Similar thin walls were achieved in the South Italian Magenta Class vases which were also made in this manner. Finger prints can be seen on the inside of the fired pottery.

The particular vases that have been discussed and illustrated are of better craftsmanship than the bulk of the pottery used by most of the population of Athens. Solid black ware and plain unglazed pottery was widely used; however, it followed the standard shapes and uses set by the finer pottery.

Chapter Two

THE GREEK BLACK GLAZE

THE DECORATION OF Attic painted vases was in the main based on the use of two colors, a reddish orange and a metallic black. The reddish orange was produced by the natural color of the fired Attic clay of the body of the vase and intensified by a surface coating of yellow ocher. The metallic black, the color of the black glaze, was made by an ingenious process from the same red Attic clay as was used for the body of the vase, and the glaze turned black during the firing operation. Accessory colors, such as white and a purplish red, were also employed, but the major colors were the painted black and the contrasting red-orange of the clay. This sophisticated, although restricted, palette was not limited as a matter of choice. These were the only pigments known to the Athenian potters that would withstand the firing of the vases.

For understanding the use of the black glaze in decorating, it is important to realize that the vases were fired only once, as was established by Gisela M. A. Richter. After the vases were formed on the wheel, they were kept in a damp room until ready to be decorated. The painting was applied directly onto the firm semi-dry or leather-hard clay surface. When the vases were completely dry, they were fired. The firing took place in three separate phases; an oxidizing, a reducing, and a reoxidizing phase.

Chemistry

The process as rediscovered by Theodor Schumann was based on the fact that the iron oxide in the Attic clay was red in color when it had been fired in an oxidizing atmosphere and black when it had been fired in a reducing atmosphere. Both the clay, which was used to form the vase, and the black glaze material, which was made from the clay, contain the same iron oxides. During the first oxidizing phase of the firing, both the vase and the glaze turned red. In the reducing phase, the vase and the glaze turned black. Then in the final reoxidizing phase, the porous fired clay of the vase again turned red, but the glaze could not reoxidize to a red color owing to the fact that it had sintered and sealed off its black iron oxide from contact with oxygen in the air. Therefore, the vase emerged from the firing red in color while the glaze remained black.

The chemistry of the process is as follows. Red ferric oxide (Fe_2O_3) is present both in the clay body of the vase and in the unfired black glaze matter. If the entire firing is done under oxidizing conditions both the vase and the glaze will turn, and remain, red. In the middle of the firing cycle, however, the oxidizing atmosphere is changed to a reducing atmosphere by the introduction of green wood or damp sawdust and closing the air vent. The smoke produced by this action is not important chemically, as smoke is largely composed of carbon which is not the coloring agent present in the Greek black glaze. The carbon is consumed in the firing at 900–950°C.

The reducing atmosphere, with the kiln closed to the outside supply of oxygen, causes incomplete combustion of the green wood or wet sawdust and produces carbon monoxide gas (CO) instead of carbon dioxide gas (CO_2) which would be developed during normal complete combustion. Carbon monoxide (CO) unites with any oxygen that it can obtain, in this case with part of the oxygen in the ferric oxide (Fe_2O_3) in the clay, turning it into ferrous oxide (FeO). This changes part of the carbon monoxide (CO) into the stable form carbon dioxide (CO_2), and the red ferric oxide (Fe_2O_3) into ferrous oxide (FeO) which is black. The reaction in this process is $Fe_2O_3 + CO = 2FeO + CO_2$. Now, the presence in the kiln of water vapor from the moisture in the pottery itself, from the green wood or wet sawdust, or perhaps from a vessel full of water placed especially in the fuel chamber, produces a magnetic oxide of iron (Fe_3O_4), which is an even blacker oxide of iron than the mere ferrous oxide (FeO). The reaction in this process is $3Fe_2O_3 + CO = 2Fe_3O_4 + CO_2$. The hydrogen from the water (H_2O) is a powerful reducing agent. If the firing cycle is stopped at this point, the clay body of the vase and the glaze will be completely and permanently black.

The process is concluded by a reoxidizing phase. Through a small hole now opened, oxygen is permitted to enter the kiln and to unite with some of the black ferrous oxide (FeO) or magnetic oxide of iron (Fe_3O_4), turning it back into the red ferric oxide (Fe_2O_3). The vase, having a porous clay body, readily allows this to happen. Consequently, the body of the vase again turns red. On the other hand, the black glazed areas, composed of either black ferrous oxide (FeO) or the black magnetic oxide of iron (Fe_3O_4), or both, do not reoxidize at these temperatures. These areas remain black, and the result of this phase is the characteristic red and black coloring of Attic vases. The glaze does not reoxidize because it becomes partly sintered and is encased in a quartz layer which does not permit the re-entry of oxygen into it and, therefore, prevents a chemical reaction from taking place (see below, this chapter). As a result, both physical and chemical factors inhibit the reversal of the process at 950°C. If the temperature is raised above 1050°C., the black oxides in the glaze will reoxidize to a red form and the black color of the glaze will be lost.

Invention

The basic technique of producing a black glaze through the three-step firing was known as early as the Middle Helladic period. Possibly the glaze was accidentally discovered when local clay was being purified. Clay, as it is dug in the pit, is almost always mixed with coarse sand, twigs, decaying vegetation, and other foreign matter. It is a simple procedure to create a suspension of clay in water and allow it to settle, separating the coarse particles and the unwanted matter from the clay. A peptizing agent such as potash, or water in which wood ashes have been soaked, might have been used to facilitate the process. It would have been good practice to coat a coarse clay vase body with a slip of a more purified clay to give it a smoother finish. The Greek kilns, fired with wood and easily capable of changing from an oxidizing to a reducing and back to a reoxidizing condition as wood was added, could accidentally have produced the first vase in this technique. An observant early potter who was willing to experiment might have worked out the process on a predictable basis.

Another possibility is that the first peptized clay slip, made of very fine particles, may have come from a stream bed where it had been formed naturally. Later, the sedimentation process would have been used to produce a similar clay slip.[1] Fundamentally, the decoration with black glaze consists of coating a vase of coarse clay with a finer layer of clay.

Even before Middle Helladic times there are examples of oxidation and reduction firing used to create red and black patterns on vases. Early in the Pottery Neolithic period, about 7,000 years ago, it was discovered that a reddish clay containing iron could be fired to either a buff-red or a gray-black color depending on whether the fire was allowed to burn freely or was smothered. Great quantities of pottery of each color were created.

Egyptian black and red ware

The earliest example of intentional use of both colors on a single vase is the Egyptian black and red ware of the third millennium BC. This particular Egyptian method was introduced on the island of Cyprus, where the same

161

161 Egyptian black and red ware.

type of black and red ware was also produced. In black and red ware, the mouth and upper part of the vase is a lustrous black and the lower section is red. The vases were made of red iron-bearing clay and were coated with a slip of red oxide of iron to heighten the red color. The entire vase was burnished, probably with an agate or jasper pebble. The floor of the kiln was covered with a deep layer of sand in which the vases were partially buried allowing only the mouths and upper portions to protrude above the sand. Then the kiln was fired in an oxidizing atmosphere to a temperature of approximately 800°C. which caused the vases to turn red. Without allowing the kiln to cool, a large quantity of green wood or dung was thrown into the kiln, which created a reducing atmosphere and carbon smudging and caused the protruding areas of the vases, including the inside unprotected by the sand, to turn black. The kiln was allowed to cool after this two-stage firing without permitting oxygen to enter. The sand was the mechanical means used to isolate the area to be left red from the area to be turned black.[2] Egyptian clay often contained a large quantity of organic material which carbonized in the firing and colored the interior of the clay body a dark gray.

Vasiliki ware

The early Minoan Vasiliki ware produced on Crete resulted from a variation *162* of this process. The decoration consists of patterns of large black spots

162 Vase from Vasiliki, Early Minoan II.

scattered over the surface of the red pottery. Perhaps the patterns were meant to imitate those on mottled stone bowls. Using the following method, I was able to reproduce this pottery. After coating the ware with a slip of yellow ocher, a form of iron oxide, the pottery was fired in the kiln in an oxidizing atmosphere. When it emerged from the kiln, it was a uniform red color. The somewhat circular black spots were added *after* the firing by holding a lighted twig of wood under the vase with the center of the body of the flame touching its surface. A single black spot resulted from the incomplete combustion in that part of the flame, reducing the iron oxide to its black form. In addition, carbon smudging penetrated the soft clay body. The surface deposit of soot was wiped off and the twig was moved to create the next spot. When a spot occurred on a strongly curved surface, the flame tended to lap around it, thus making a curved spot. The result of the licking action of the flame indicates the position in which the pot was held. A red center could be added to a black spot by holding the burning twig lower so that only the tip of the flame touched the spot. This part of the flame is oxidizing and will change the black iron oxide to its red form and will consume the carbon smudging. The yellow color which surrounds some of the black spots was caused by partial reduction. An examination of the surface of a Vasiliki vase under low magnification reveals that the ocher wash in the areas of the black or red spots is cracked and crazed, differing markedly from the balance of the vase. This damage is due to the intense local surface heating.

If a fragment of the ware is subjected to refiring in an oxidizing atmosphere at a temperature of 900°C., the black iron oxide will reoxidize to a red color and the carbon smudging will burn off, leaving the fragment totally red. Only the small cracks in the ocher wash will show the location of the vanished black spots.

In decorating the vase, the spots were made one at a time, either small, large, or overlapping, by moving the burning twig. They could be spaced singly or in groups utilizing some rudimentary elements of design. Fine details, of course, could not be rendered by this process.[3]

Dimini ware

Not all early pottery from Greece was decorated with a black or red glaze colored by means of an oxide of iron. For example, Dimini ware (a Neolithic pottery from Thessaly), some types of Middle Helladic pottery from Aegina, and Geometric pottery from Cyprus, were decorated with brown and black lines colored by natural mineral pigments, such as manganese, which required only a single-stage firing rather than the three-stage firing needed to produce the black color in Attic pottery.[4] The lines and areas decorated with these natural pigments usually have a dull matte surface. This may be contrasted to the black glaze made with an oxide of iron which has a slight sheen.

Terminology

The term, *glaze*, has been widely used to describe the black color on Attic pottery. Yet in some ways it is a misnomer. Potters today use the term glaze for a substance containing sufficient silica and various fluxes which act upon the silica to cause the mixture to fuse and bring about a "glassy" surface. This does not hold true for the Greek black glaze. Although there is a substantial amount of silica in the black glaze, the amount is comparable to that in the clay body. At temperatures between 825°C. and 945°C., the glaze does not completely melt. Instead, the glaze enters a transitional stage known as sintering. The black glaze matter is applied to a vessel in the form of a clay slip, or engobe, which is then heated in the firing until it sinters. Perhaps it would be more accurate to refer to it as a sintered engobe or some other term which would take into consideration the metallic luster of the sintered surface, but the term "black glaze" is not entirely incorrect, and can be used as long as the origin is fully understood. On the other hand the coating should never be referred to as black paint.

Composition

Table II compares the composition of the clay body and the black glaze of a fragment of a foot from a fifth-century BC vase found on the outskirts of the Agora in Athens. This comparison shows that the clay body and black glaze are basically the same with a higher concentration of the heavier minerals in the glaze. Every element found in substantial quantity in the black glaze is also present in the clay body, which bears out the findings of Dr Schumann and other researchers who stipulated that the color of the black glaze was not created by the addition of a special ingredient or pigment.

Preparation

In order to study the methods of decoration of Attic pottery, it was necessary to duplicate the ancient black glaze and accessory colors. The preparation of a black glaze is based on the reports of Schumann, Winter, and Farnsworth. Several years of experimentation brought about some modifications. In one pint of distilled water dissolve $2\frac{1}{2}$ grams of Calgon (sodium hexametaphosphate), $(NaPO_3)_6$. Calgon is the peptizing or deflocculating agent. When it is thoroughly dissolved, mix completely into the solution 4 ounces by weight of damp Attic clay.[5] This mixture is allowed to stand in a tall glass container for 48 hours. During this time, it separates into three clearly recognizable areas. At the top, a substantial quantity of very fine particles of clay is suspended in a colloidal suspension. Between this top colloidal zone and the bottom zone, there is a clearly visible area of clay slip composed of particles of average size. At the bottom there are sand and coarser particles which were present in the clay. The top colloidal suspension of fine particles is carefully removed with a siphon for further preparation of the black glaze. The middle zone may be used in making the clay body of a vase. The bottom zone is discarded.

The suspension of fine particles has to be thickened by evaporation. Either the water is allowed to evaporate over a period of several weeks or the solution can be boiled down without injury. Evaporation is continued until the liquid has the consistency of very heavy cream. This constitutes the glaze slip with which the Attic vases were decorated. The unfired glaze preparation is of a deep brown tone, darker than the plain Attic clay. It already possesses, when dry, a slightly metallic sheen. Glaze matter which does not possess this metallic sheen in the dry state, will not fire black, but will turn red in the same way as does the unglazed clay body.

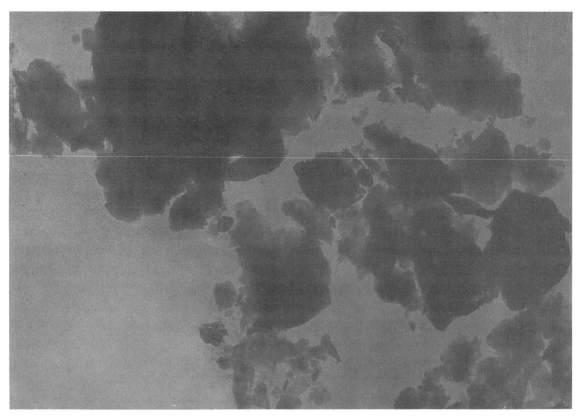

163 *Attic red clay, 5,000x.*

Examination by electron microscope

The effect of the separation or deflocculation process can be studied with an electron microscope which is capable of much higher magnification than a conventional light microscope. A sample of purified red Attic clay from Amarousi and a sample of unfired black glaze matter made from the same clay by the separation process described above were examined under the electron microscope by Mr H. M. Allred of the Texaco Research Center, Beacon, New York, and the following description is based on his microscopic examination.

Several attempts were made to prepare specimens of each of the clay samples from dilute water suspensions, but a satisfactory dispersion of particles upon the specimen screen could not be obtained because the particles tended to flocculate. Consequently, petroleum ether was chosen as a suspension medium. Small amounts of each of the clays were shaken with petroleum ether to make very dilute suspensions. Droplets of each of these suspensions were then deposited on several plastic film (polyvinyl formal) coated specimen grids and allowed to dry. These specimens were then

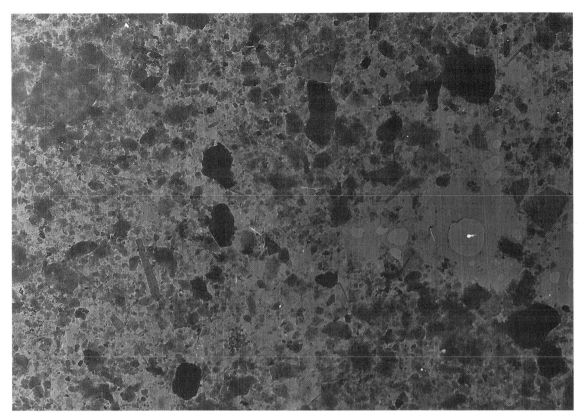

164 *Modern Attic black glaze material, 13,000x.*

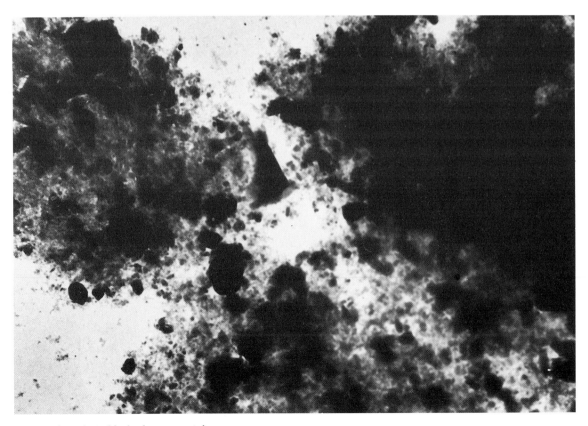

165 *Modern Attic black glaze material, 77,000x.*

examined in an RCA type EMU$_2$ electron microscope and electron micrographs were obtained of areas that appeared representative of the clay dispersion. The micrographs of the Attic red clay were taken at an electronic magnification of 1,000X. The micrographs of the modern Greek black glaze material were taken at magnifications of 2,900X and 17,500X. Photographic enlargements were made from the electron microscope plates and the total magnification of each print is shown in its caption.

163   In ill. 163 can be seen the large particles and aggregates of particles that appear to characterize the red Attic clay. The largest particles observed in the micrographs taken of this material were as much as ten microns across. These large particles are of irregular shape. There are smaller particles of material present in the sample as well.

164   Ill. 164 shows that the sample of modern Greek black glaze material is composed of much smaller particles. The largest particles observed were thin platelets not larger than two microns across. The average particle size appears to be in the range of a few tenths of a micron, although examination of the material at high magnification shows the presence of exceedingly fine material having dimensions in the order of a few hundredths of a micron. It

165   will be noted that the majority of the particles seen in ill. 165 appear to be platelets. Some of these platelets are sufficiently thin to be relatively transparent to the electron beam, a factor which permits smaller underlying particles to be observed. It is conceivable that, when a thick suspension of this material is brushed onto the surface of a pottery vessel, these platelets could be preferentially oriented in such a way that firing would result in the sintering of the sheets to form a surface relatively impervious to oxygen during the reoxidation step of the firing process.

Spectrographic analysis

A spectrographic analysis of a modern Attic clay and modern black glaze is given in Table III. Again there are great similarities between the glaze and the clay with a noticeable concentration of the heavier elements in the glaze. This glaze was made from the same clay that was analyzed. Compare Table III with Table II for the same tests on the ancient and modern Attic clays and black glazes and notice the similarities.

The glaze matter may be dried and later prepared for use whenever desired by the addition of water. Once the black glaze matter has been dried it can be stored indefinitely. I have kept it for 25 years, then added water, and it produced a fine black glaze on pottery. It is possible that Attic black glaze matter was exported to Greek colonies in ancient times in this form. Probably this would have been only a temporary expedient until an adequate clay supply was found. The use of a glaze made from a clay of different quality than that used for the body of the vase is not desirable, because the two components may have different coefficients of expansion. During firing and cooling, the glaze and the body should expand and contract at the same rate. If they do not react uniformly, stresses occur which cause cracking and, ultimately, flaking of the glaze. Modern potters term this balance between the glaze and the body as the "fit" of the glaze, and in modern practice it can be adjusted by additives in the glaze. The ancient potters did not have this control and achieved their best results when the black glaze matter was made from the same clay as was used for the body of the vase. A glaze made from a different clay could be used if by chance it had the same coefficient of expansion as the vase body.

Not all iron-bearing clays are suitable for the manufacture of the black glaze.[6] The electron micrographs show that the separation of very tiny particles of clay is necessary, though the specific chemical process was not known. Nor was the mechanism understood which causes the black glaze to form at about 825°C. and remain intact up to about 1050°C. at which time it reoxidizes to a red color. This phase of the study was undertaken by Mr P. H. Lewis, also of the Texaco Research Laboratories, Beacon, New York. The following is based on his chemical report.

Examination by x-ray diffraction

An x-ray diffraction study determines the chemical compounds that are present in a scraping from a pottery surface. This yields more information than a spectrographic study which tells only what elements are present in a sample. The results of an x-ray analysis of a sample is a series of lines on a photographic film. It is the position of these lines and their intensity that are used to identify the chemical compounds present. A perfectly successful x-ray analysis permits an exact correlation of the lines on the x-ray photograph with those in a standard compilation. Unfortunately, the x-ray examination of silicates often yields x-ray photographs for which exact correlation to known x-ray results becomes impossible. This is because complex silicates are not pure, but contain dissolved foreign elements and compounds which affect the x-ray diffraction lines. Despite this lack of exact correlation of observed to standard x-ray lines, sufficient correlation does exist so that a reasonable estimate can be made as to the identification of an unknown compound.

Specimens of Attic red illite clay found at Amarousi, modern black glaze material, fragments of ancient Attic black glazed pottery from the Acropolis, the Agora, and the Ceramicus, were examined. The mineral celadonite was found to be the source of the iron in the Attic red clay, its chemical formula being $(K, Ca_{\frac{1}{2}}, Na)_{0.84} (Al_{0.34}Fe^{III}_{0.76}Fe^{II}_{0.24}Mg_{0.76}) (Si_{3.84}Al_{0.11}) O_{10} (OH)_2$.

Heating in the kiln causes the clay to decompose into an iron compound and quartz. The quartz that is formed can do one of two things. The first is to form new crystals of quartz. The second is to add on to existing crystals of quartz. It is the first process, the nucleation of new crystals of quartz, that permits inclusions of iron silicates. Once these are formed, the iron is cut off from exposure to the atmosphere and cannot be reoxidized to the red form.

A mechanism for the black coloration of the pottery that requires mica to sinter to encapsulate iron oxides seems to be untenable. The scrapings from neither the ancient nor the modern fired glazes contain appreciable amounts of mica.

It must be concluded that the black coloration is due to "iron" trapped in a layer of quartz. The form of the iron may differ from sample to sample but can be iron metal, $(Mg, Fe) SiO_3$, or tiny crystals of iron entrapped in the quartz (not observable by x-ray diffraction).

Magnetic test

The presence of iron in the form of Fe_3O_4, the black magnetic oxide of iron, can also be demonstrated by using a powdered sample of black glaze and an electromagnet. The magnet will readily pick up the powdered iron-bearing glaze, and when the current in the magnet is switched off, the powdered glaze will fall.

The preparation of a sample of black glaze for this type of experiment can be done by scraping the glaze from an Attic sherd with a sharp knife. In testing a modern reproduction of the black glaze, it is easier to allow a sample of glaze matter to dry on a glass plate. When dry, it will readily separate from the glass and the flakes may be put into a porcelain cup for firing in the kiln. This method not only saves the labor of scraping the sample from the clay body, but insures a pure specimen uncontaminated by small particles of the clay adhering to the glaze.

Suitable clay

When the iron is trapped by the formation of the quartz at about 825°C., it is held isolated from contact with the surrounding air so that it cannot reoxidize. If, however, the temperature is increased to about 1050°C., the quartz layer softens and allows oxygen to penetrate the glaze where it readily reoxidizes the black ferrous oxide to ferric oxide which is red in color. Therefore, Attic clay, suitable for the manufacture of black glaze, contains celadonite which supplies the iron and quartz in the proper forms. Some of the particles of the clay are platelets small enough to be separated from the balance of the clay by the deflocculating process. Apparently the thin platelets which are observed in the electron micrographs of the black glaze material become preferentially oriented in the drying and burnishing of the glaze surface so that they form a laminated layer. This would account for the metallic sheen of the dried glaze. In firing, the platelets readily sinter owing to their extreme thinness and alignment. Water vapor from the clay or from another source introduced into the kiln during firing appears to aid in the formation of the black glaze, perhaps by lowering the temperature at which these reactions take place.

The studies of F. Oberlies and N. Köppen substantiate the importance of the alignments of the platelets.[7] They made a series of microscopic photographs of cross-sections of black glaze samples, and electron micrographs of the surface of similar samples. It was determined that the smaller the particle size in the black glaze matter, the better the platelets were aligned. The smallest aligned platelets produced the best sintered layers in the glaze in firing. The most uniform layers with a smooth outer surface produced the best black glaze with a high surface luster.[8]

The production of the Greek black glaze required a high degree of technical proficiency and accurate standardization of manufacturing procedures. In the fourth century BC the loss of Athens' foreign markets, the change of interest by its artists to other forms of expression, and the increasing popularity of metal and glass vessels, caused a decline in the output and quality of Attic vases. Although the black glaze continued to be used on plain vases and those decorated with molded patterns in relief, it, too, declined in quality. This was due to the lack of control of the size of the platelets in the glaze. Larger plates produced a duller glaze.

Export of technique

The black glaze had been carried by trade and by Greek colonists to southern Italy where it was employed by the Etruscans and later by the Apulians, the Campanians, and others. One of the most important centers for the production of pottery in Italy in the fourth century BC was the city of Tarentum. Vast quantities of South Italian vases of the Apulian style were made there and decorated with the Greek black glaze. Through the co-

166 Etruscan bucchero kantharos, seventh century B.C.

operation of Pietro Anti, a potter in Grottaglie, a town near the site of ancient Tarentum, I obtained a sample of local clay in order to determine its suitability for the manufacture of black glaze. It produced a glaze of good quality which resembled that used on ancient South Italian vases.

Bucchero ware

Before the introduction of the black glaze the Etruscans employed a controlled firing technique in the manufacture of their entirely black pottery known as bucchero ware. This ware was made from an iron-bearing clay, which they fired under reducing conditions at a temperature of about 800°C. The pottery was colored black from the reduction of the iron oxide and from carbon smudging.[9]

Terra Sigillata

During Roman times, the black glaze was widely used throughout the Mediterranean region, and when it was fired in only an oxidizing atmo-

166

sphere, it became a fine red glaze. The so-called "Megarian" bowls, produced in many areas of the Eastern Mediterranean starting at the end of the third century BC, were first made with a black glaze and then graduated to a predominance of red ware. This was followed by the red "Pergamene" and "Samian" pottery which was also made at various locations. The most famous ware, and the ware of the highest quality, was the Arretine pottery made at Arretium in Italy from about 30 BC to AD 30.[10] It is a type of red glaze relief molded ware, often referred to as *terra sigillata*, or "earthenware decorated with small figures."

167

The technique of these black and red glazes spread across Europe to Gaul and Roman Britain. One of the main centers of production in the second century AD was Lezoux in central Gaul. Eventually, in the disintegration of the Roman Empire, the Greek black glaze was lost, and was superseded by a ceramic glaze introduced from the Eastern Mediterranean. A glassy type of glaze most commonly used by potters today, it consists of silica and a flux, colored with mineral additives. The ceramic glaze has been widely and

167 Arretine krater, signed by [M. Perennius] Tigranus as owner of the pottery. This type of red glaze relief molded ware is often referred to as 'terra sigillata'.

continuously employed since its invention because it is easy to use with little chance for failure, and it offers an unlimited choice of colors.

Plumbate ware

Although the use of the Greek black glaze ultimately was abandoned in late Roman times, it is interesting to note that a basically similar glaze was independently invented in Central America in pre-Columbian times. It was used on the Mesoamerican pottery known as plumbate ware.[11] The name plumbate, derived from the Roman word for lead, *plumbum*, is a misnomer. Although on many specimens the gray glaze exhibits a leaden color, it does not result from the use of lead. Technically, the plumbate glaze is very similar to the Greek black glaze, though it is not so fine in quality. The many color variations range from a near black to almost a *terra sigillata* red, probably as a result of a lack of control, principally in the firing. The plumbate glaze has the same metallic sheen and the very hard surface of the Greek black glaze. In plumbate ware, the glaze is used to cover the entire pot with what was intended to be a uniform tone, and it was not used to draw figures or patterns. The decoration of the vessels consisted of incised lines, stamped and impressed patterns, freehand modeling, and molded appliqués. The ware appears to have been fired at a temperature of about 950°C., comparable to the Greek black glaze.

Modern usage

The Greek black glaze has been reproduced by many experimenters since the pioneering work of Theodor Schumann in 1942, but it has not been used commercially, owing to the difficulties of firing and uncertainties of results. The nearest related process in limited use today applies a coating of a colloidal suspension of red clay slip, rich in iron, to a small variety of craft products in order to give them a more handsome color resembling that of *terra sigillata*.[12]

The rediscovery of the technique of producing the Greek black glaze makes it possible for a forger to create a modern vase from Attic clay using a black glaze that is chemically identical to that of a genuine Attic vase. Obviously, it became necessary to devise a method of differentiating between such a forgery and an ancient vase. The examination of the glaze surfaces under high magnification appeared to offer such a method. Accordingly, this study was undertaken by H. M. Allred. The following account is based on his report.

Differences between ancient and modern black glaze

Portions of the black glaze surface of the pottery were examined by both light and electron microscopy. The light micrographs of these surfaces were obtained through the use of a Bausch and Lomb Tri-vert Illuminator. This is a device that provides a variety of near vertical illumination (called epi-illumination) of the surface to be examined. It was found that the best definition of the surface roughness of the pottery sherds was obtained when the dark-field stop of the illuminator was in the light beam. The micrographs were made of each surface at 11.8x initial magnification on the negatives which were further enlarged photographically.

The pottery glaze was examined electron microscopically through the use of surface replica techniques. The micrographs illustrated were obtained from Faxfilm-carbon two-step replicas which were prepared as follows.

Faxfilm is a cellulose acetate sheet. It was softened with a suitable solvent and pressed against the surface that was to be replicated. After it had dried in contact with the surface, it was peeled readily from that surface and carried with it a negative replica of the surface structure. This film was too thick, however, to examine directly in the electron microscope. Consequently, another film that was thin enough to be examined directly in the electron microscope was deposited on the surface of the Faxfilm replica. This secondary film was produced by condensing, in a vacuum, a thin layer of carbon evaporated from an arc onto the Faxfilm replica surface. To emphasize the irregularities on the surface of the carbon replica, a shadow layer was deposited by evaporation, at an angle to the surface of the replica. A small amount of platinum or of tungsten oxide was deposited onto the Faxfilm before the carbon film was formed. The replica was then cut into small squares of a size suitable for examination in the electron microscope, and the Faxfilm dissolved away from the carbon in acetone, leaving the carbon to be transferred to the specimen support screens for examination in the electron microscope. When the Faxfilm was dissolved, the metal remained on the carbon film.

The presentation of the electron micrographs is that of a negative replica. That is, any pits that were in the pottery surface will appear as protrusions on the surface of the replica. The light areas of the prints correspond to shadows behind these dark protrusions on the metal shadowed replica.

The light micrographs in ills 168, 169 are of a portion of the surface of the *168, 169* modern black glaze taken from the dot in the eye of a figure on a pottery reproduction. Ill. 168 shows this dot and the surrounding tooling and glaze at

26X magnification. When a portion of this dot was examined at a higher magnification, 160X (ill. 169), the surface appeared relatively smooth and showed iridescent colors such as are sometimes observed on glassy clinkers or slag. These bands of coloration appear as parallel lines of color to the eye, and are apparent at the lower right. The circular image at the center of the micrograph apparently resulted from a bubble in the glaze. The bottom of the pit was not in focus in the microscope. The area represented in ill. 169 is just below the center of ill. 168 where this bubble can be seen.

170 Ill. 170 shows an electron micrograph at 11,000X magnification, illustrating the degree of smoothness, on an electron microscopic scale, of the glaze surface of the modern reproduction. In general, the surface was somewhat irregular, but without sharply defined irregularities. There were, however, areas on the glaze that were extremely smooth, broken only by the presence of irregular mesas or sinks. This micrograph shows a surface that is typical of the surface of glass and suggests that a glassy surface or glaze is produced in these areas when the pottery is fired.

171–173 Ills 171–173 are light and electron micrographs of the black surface of a pottery sherd from the Acropolis in Athens. Similar micrographs, not illustrated, were obtained from sherds from the Agora and the Ceramicus. These micrographs are self-explanatory and it will be observed in comparing ills 172, 173 with the corresponding light micrographs from the reproduction (ills 168, 169) that the surface of the genuine black glaze is very rough compared with the surface of the modern reproduction. The parallel striations are undoubtedly brush marks and the pitted character of the surface, which is reminiscent of the surface of glass that has long been soaked in acid dichromate cleaning solution, no doubt resulted from centuries of leaching action by the ground water in the environment in which the pottery sherd had been buried. Note the differences between ill. 172 and ill. 173. The first is of the convex surface of the sherd and the second is of the concave surface. The convex surface, which is assumed to be the outside of a vessel, is much rougher than the concave surface, suggesting that the exterior of this vessel before it was broken and buried was subjected to a much more corrosive atmosphere or weathering than the interior.

The electron micrograph of the sherd from the Acropolis (ill. 171) shows the finer details of the surface roughness, including considerable pitting and etching. In principle, the difference in surface quality allows one to differentiate between antiquities (ill. 171), and modern reproductions (ill. 170), through the use of light and electron microscopy.

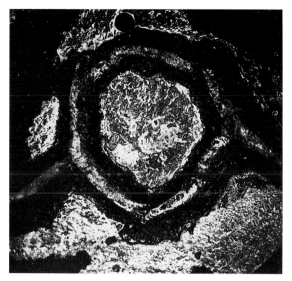

168 *Surface of modern Attic black glaze, 26x.*

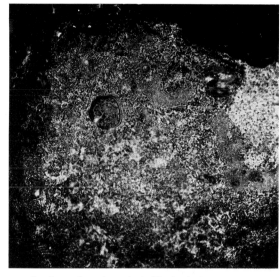

169 *Surface of modern Attic black glaze, 160x.*

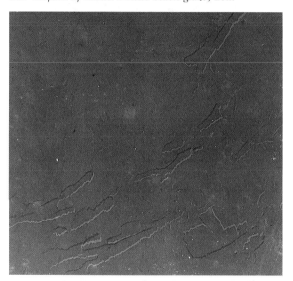

170 *Surface of modern Attic black glaze, 11,000x.*

171 *Surface of ancient Attic black glaze, 11,000x.*

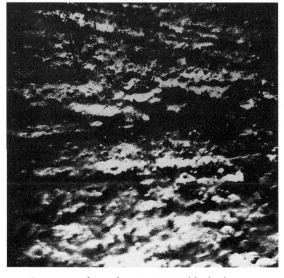

172 *Convex surface of ancient Attic black glaze, 26x.*

173 *Concave surface of ancient Attic black glaze, 26x.*

174 *Red-figure vase-painting by the Berlin Painter, early fifth century* BC. *An entertainer playing a kithara. See ill.* 205.

Chapter Three

DECORATING THE VASES

THE DESTRUCTION OF THE Mycenaean culture during the twelfth century BC, including the loss of the pottery techniques, caused a dark age from which Greek ceramics emerged anew about 1000 BC. The decoration of the new Attic pottery was based on geometric patterns which covered the ware with bands, concentric circles, and angular arrangements. By the eighth century BC human figures, drawn as simple linear silhouettes, were introduced into this *175* Geometric style. In the following Proto-Attic period the emphasis shifted from the decorative patterns to the figures which were drawn in a more na- *177* turalistic outline technique. The potters of Corinth in the seventh century BC developed the incised line adding detail and decisive clarity to their black glaze silhouette figures. From these techniques Athenian potters synthesized the Attic black-figure style by the end of the seventh century. Over the next 100 years, Athenian technology and artistic ability enabled Attic pottery to *176,1* become unsurpassed in all Greece.[1]

Shortly after the middle of the sixth century BC, an Athenian potter invented a device which produced black glaze lines in relief. This made possible delicate black lines sharply contrasting against the red clay background. About 530 BC the vase-painting technique was reversed, perhaps as a result of the pioneering efforts of the Andokides Painter. Instead of painting the figures as black silhouettes with incised details, the figures were outlined and interior details were added using the relief line. Then the entire background around the figures was painted black. This red-figure style created a more realistic effect, for it presented human figures in the light red *174,205,II* color of the clay against a dark glaze background. For a generation, both black-figure and red-figure flourished side by side; however, the new technique eventually largely superseded the old. Although red-figure was paramount, black-figure continued as a trickle beside the main stream. A silhouette technique without the incised line was used occasionally on red-figured vases, and the traditional black-figure decoration was retained on

175 *Geometric vase-painting, eighth century* BC. *Human figures are drawn as simple linear silhouettes.*

176 *Black-figure vase-painting by the Amasis Painter, about* 550 BC.

177 Proto-Attic vase-painting, 670–650 BC. This shows a technique intermediate between those of ills. 175 and 176.

Panathenaic amphorae at least into Hellenistic times. Red-figure vase-painting continued in Athens until the last quarter of the fourth century BC when it was abandoned.[2] Subsequently, relief-molded pottery, made in imitation of metal bowls, and other techniques became popular. The Athenian style and technique of vase decoration was copied in Italy, first by *III, IV* the Etruscans, and later by the Greek colonies.

Subjects

The subjects of the scenes represented on Attic vases also underwent an evolutionary development. The black-figured ware of the sixth century utilized to the fullest extent the rich lore of Attic mythology. Gods and goddesses, heroes and monsters, illustrated the stories of Olympus and the Trojan War. Decorative elements such as the palmette, lotus, and meander were used to frame the panels in which the black-figure scenes were painted. Gradually, the theme of mortal man acting out his daily life was introduced. The soldier arming for battle, the activities in the gymnasium, and the carousing in drunken revels began to supersede the divine myths.

This tendency continued in the fifth and fourth centuries in the decoration of the red-figured vases. Humanism became paramount, although mythological subjects continued to be used to a lesser degree. Battles, banquets, and athletic contests were drawn, as were the daily chores of weaving, bathing, and dressing within the home. Real people were shown performing the real tasks of daily life, less heroic perhaps, but a faithful portrayal of reality. Decorative elements were subsidiary; they were used to set off the drawing, or to add interest to the mouth or other parts of the vase which the artist wished to emphasize.

Sketches

Undoubtedly a vase-painter evolved some of his compositions, particularly the complicated designs, by making trial sketches before he began work on a vase. None has survived, unfortunately, as they were apparently made on a perishable material like plaques of unfired clay, wax tablets, or wooden boards primed with white pigment. Perhaps these sketches were kept for a few years by the painter to add to his repertoire but, since the vases had strongly curved surfaces and varying shapes, a sketch on a flat surface was of limited value. The final design had to be adapted to harmonize with the shape of the vase, and fitted to the curvature of the area. Therefore, the painter probably created most compositions working directly on the vase, and it may have been that finished vases, decorated with various subjects, were kept by each pottery establishment to serve as sales samples to show to customers. Such sample vases also would have been used by the potters and the painters as a library of shapes and subjects.

The vase-painters sketched their subjects on the surface of the semi-dry or leather-hard vases probably with a thin pointed stick of charcoal or lead. Occasionally, the vase was not as dry as it should have been, or the painter pressed too hard, so the stick left slightly indented lines which were preserved when the vase was fired. These indented "sketch lines" are visible on *178–180* numerous vases, both black-figured and red-figured.[3] The painters often sketched their figures nude and then drew clothes over them in order to render their movement correctly. The charcoal or lead lines which were clearly visible to the painter vanished in the firing process.

The tondo of a red-figured cup in Vienna by the Epidromos Painter exhibits an unusual sketch indented beneath the final painted scene.[4] The sketch is of a naked running youth, while the finished scene is of Hermes leading an animal. Apparently, the Epidromos Painter first sketched the youth, changed his mind about his subject, turned the cup around 180° in his hand, and drew another subject, Hermes and the animal, which appears upside down on top of his first sketch. The drawing of Hermes was more pleasing to him so he painted it. However, after the firing, the original sketch of the running youth still showed beneath the superimposed painted scene of Hermes and the animal. A similar instance occurs on a red-figured cup in the manner of the Antiphon Painter in The Metropolitan Museum of Art. The original sketch was of a horse and a man which the painter discarded in favor of a discobolus.[5]

Procedure

The working procedure of a black-figure vase-painter is visible on an *181* amphora in New York. After making sketch lines, he outlined his figures in black glaze before filling in an area. Then with his compass he incised a large circle which was to be a shield and which he was going to paint with a white clay slip. He filled in the upper and lower parts of the body of the warrior with black glaze but did not fill in the torso; the torso section was to be covered by the white shield. Before painting with the white slip, he incised three balls for

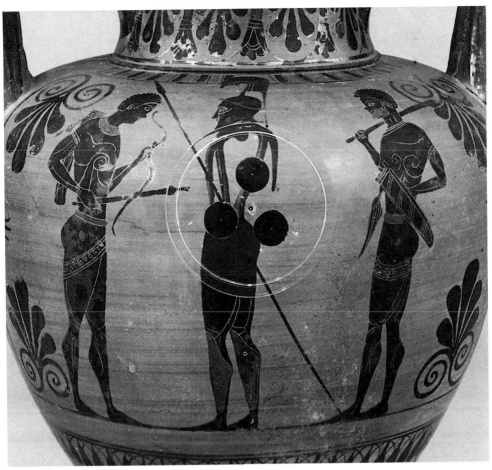

181 Black-figure sketch of the torso of a warrior, by a painter near Exekias. Possibly the subject is Memnon between two Ethiopians.

the shield device with his compass and painted them black. Next, the white slip was painted on the shield area covering the outline of the torso of the warrior. Added white slip has a tendency to flake, which it did in this case, revealing the torso sketch.

The standard black-figure technique required figures to be rendered a solid black tone; however, a black outline style, descended from the Proto-Attic, was used sparingly. Ultimately, the outline style achieved widespread usage on white-ground vases.

In the best red-figure painting, after the sketch lines were drawn, the artist usually outlined the figures with a painted broad contour band of black glaze, sometimes called the "eighth-inch stripe," which served as a guard against overlapping while painting the black areas. Next, the details of the figures

182,183 Interior and exterior views of an unfinished Campanian kylix, showing red-figure vasepainting. It appears to have been fired as a test piece.

184 Unfinished red-figure vase-painting, by the Painter of Bologna 228; the three figures are outlined in black glaze, the interior relief lines omitted.

were drawn with the relief line and dilute glaze as described later in this chapter. A kylix, apparently broken while being decorated, clearly shows this *182, 183* sequence. It was preserved in an unfinished condition as it was fired as a test piece instead of being discarded.

Another unfinished vase also illustrates this sequence. Probably owing to an oversight, the painter did not finish one side of a column krater, and left three figures outlined in black glaze and omitted the interior relief lines. *184*

Duplicates

The painters did not trace their compositions even when they were duplicating them. Ills 185, 186 show how the painter has reproduced the *185, 186* identical scene on both sides of a pelike. Close examination reveals many

185,186 Details of red-figure on a pelike; the reverse of the vase (opposite) shows a probable copy of the initial painting on the obverse. By a painter near the Pig Painter.

differences between sides A and B. Side A (ill. 185) was probably painted first, as the painter drew it in greater detail and more carefully. Side B (ill. 186) would have been the freehand copy.

Entire vases were duplicated freehand, as in a pair of kylikes by Aristophanes in the Museum of Fine Arts, Boston. The tondos and exteriors of both cups are the same, the Centauromachy at the wedding-feast of Perithous, with only minor variations in the rendering.[6]

187,188   An even more interesting example is an amphora in Boston.[7] It is a so-called "bilingual" vase in which one side is decorated in the black-figure technique

and the other in red-figure. The same subject, Herakles driving a bull to sacrifice, appears on both sides. There are numerous variations between the two drawings demonstrating that one side was not traced from the other. The vase was made in the last quarter of the sixth century BC and graphically illustrates the coexistence of the older black-figure technique and the newly invented red-figure. A careful study of the two sides of this vase is very instructive because it clearly illustrates the strengths and weaknesses of the two techniques. The modifications of the drawing and the rendering of the details show how the technique dictated the manner of execution.

187,188 A "bilingual" amphora. One side is decorated in black-figure by the Lysippides Painter; the reverse side (opposite) in red-figure by the Andokides Painter.

Tools

A few simple tools were used by the painters, among them the caliper. Both potters and painters used the caliper to transfer and compare measurements. A pair of calipers can be seen hanging on the wall over the boy turning the wheel in the pottery in ills 1, 6. The compass, a modification of the caliper, was used to draw circles, as for shields and chariot wheels on many black-figured vases. A combination straightedge and ruler was used for measuring and drawing straight lines. Such an instrument is shown hanging on the wall next to the caliper.

    In both the black-figure and red-figure periods, the brush was used to paint solid areas, figures, and designs on the vases. The ancient paint brush very closely resembled those in use today. Often the black glaze was applied to the vase while it turned on the wheel, permitting both a smooth application over

large areas, such as the interior of bowls, and ease in making bands. The areas around handles, of course, were painted when the vase was stationary.

Black-figure decoration

A sequence in the making of the copy of the black-figured kylix demonstrates the method of decoration. A thin base coat of yellow ocher to intensify the color of the clay body is brushed over the vase. This is polished to achieve a very smooth surface which will increase the luster of the glaze. The black glaze matter is applied with a broad brush to the areas intended to be black and the details of design are drawn with a fine brush. The added red slip and white slip are also applied with a fine brush. Finally, the incised lines are engraved with a sharp point, and the vase is then ready for firing. The details of these steps are discussed later in this chapter.

189–202

189 An ocher wash is applied to the entire vase with a brush.

190 The ocher will intensify the reddish color of the clay.

191 The ocher is burnished with an agate pebble.

192 Burnishing consolidates and polishes the surface.

193 Black glaze matter is applied with a brush.

194 The vase is rotated to obtain a uniform coating of glaze.

195 *Decorative elements are painted with a fine brush.*

196 *Lines are sketched in with lead, and added red is applied over the black glaze.*

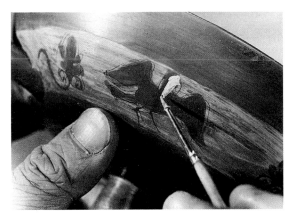

197 *Added white is applied last.*

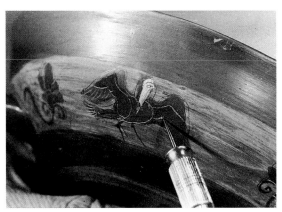

198 *Incision is made with a sharp point.*

199 *After drying, the kylix is ready for firing.*

200 *After firing, the kylix is finished.*

201 *Compare with ill. 193; note the black circle.*

202 *Compare with ill. 199; note the intensified colors.*

Mistakes

When damp, the unfired black glaze matter is quite close in color to the background clay body making it difficult to see what one is painting under these conditions. Thus, it is possible that the vase-painters of antiquity added some form of fugitive vegetable coloring to the black glaze matter in order to make it contrast with the clay at the time of painting. On the other hand, certain mistakes made by vase-painters indicate that they found it difficult to distinguish between painted and unpainted areas. Some vases show drops of glaze spilled on the drawing area. Occasionally, the brush has gone over an area which should have remained blank and, conversely, some areas have been left unglazed by mistake. These errors could have been rectified easily if they could have been seen, but evidently such was not the case.

It would have been possible to make erasures before firing to change designs and correct mistakes. If the glaze was still damp, errors were removed with a moist sponge. Often this left a telltale brown smudge quite noticeable in corrections of lettering. Dry glaze was removed by scraping which caused a slightly roughened area. Incised lines were an added problem if a black-figure vase-painter changed his mind about a composition. Under each handle of a small neck-amphora, now in the Cooper Union Museum in New York, the painter incised a geometric pattern with his compass. Patterns were not employed under the handles on this type of amphora, so the logical explanation is that they were doodles intended for shield devices. He covered the designs with black glaze; but the incising shows through the glaze.[8] The Kleophrades Painter decided to change the position of a shield on a calyx krater now in The Metropolitan Museum of Art.[9] He covered the shield with clay slip to obtain a new surface and then drew the second shield. The added clay slip flaked, unfortunately, thus revealing the unwanted shield first painted. The painter of a red-figured lekythos now in Boston wished to change a meander band he had drawn and covered it with black glaze. The applied coating was too thin and transparent so the band can still be seen.

203

204

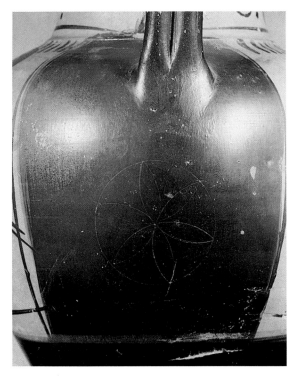

203 Detail of a neck-amphora, doubleen near the Edinburgh Painter, showing an incised pattern painted over with black glaze.

204 Detail of a lekythos which shows an unwanted meander band thinly painted over with black glaze.

205 Detail of amphora shown in ill. 174. The relief lines forming the strings of the kithara stand out from the background glaze.

Red-figure decoration

Scenes on Greek vases of potters and painters at work, while rare, do exist and are useful in the study of vase-painting techniques.[10] The most representative scene extant of Attic vase-painters at work appears on a red-figured hydria, now in the Torno collection in Milan. This vase has often been described and illustrated.[11] Four painters are shown: a man, two youths, and a woman. The two vase-painters on the left side of the panel are each shown with two cups beside them containing the glaze matter which they paint on the vase. The youth on the right side of the panel has a single cup of glaze matter, and the glaze cup used by the woman is not visible as it is apparently on the other side of her body where it would be convenient to her right hand as she paints the

206 Detail of ill. 2. The vase-painter is working on decorative patterns which were done with a brush.

vase. One of the two cups used by each of the two painters on the left side of the panel has a lid.

The reason for two vase-painters each having two cups of glaze would appear to be that they contain glazes of different consistency. One cup presumably contains thinner black glaze matter, the consistency of heavy cream, and the other cup contains a much thicker black glaze substance which is used to produce the Attic relief line widely used in red-figured ware. The cup containing the very thick glaze matter is the one that would require the lid to prevent further evaporation and caking.

An examination of Attic vases bears out this explanation. In examples where the black relief line goes over the black background glaze, the use of two glazes of different consistencies is clearly shown. Ills 174, 205 illustrate *174,205* an example on a red-figured amphora by the Berlin Painter in The Metropolitan Museum of Art.[12] The relief lines forming the strings of the kithara stand out from the background glaze. Note that six line segments make up each of the spirals. We know that on the background, thin black glaze was applied with a brush, because in certain cases the brush marks can easily be seen. Sometimes two coats of glaze, which can be observed if one looks carefully, were used to cover the vase. In vase-paintings showing a painter at work, a brush is often shown grasped in the hand of the painter. Unfortunately, the illustrations of vase-painters at work show them drawing only decorative elements or filling in the solid background areas. On the *2,206* hydria, two of the male vase-painters are shown working on decorative patterns which were always done with a brush. The woman is shown painting the solid area between the handles of a volute krater with a brush, and the principal vase-painter is poised with a brush about to begin a pattern on the lower part of the bowl of a large kantharos. All are shown grasping a brush in their fists with the bristles downward in the oriental manner, but none is shown doing figures or ornaments that would require the relief line.

Relief line

There are no ancient illustrations of a vase-painter drawing a relief line. The nearest thing to the representation for which we are looking occurs on a red-*207* figured kylix fragment in the Museum of Fine Arts in Boston.[13] In the fingers of his right hand the painter is holding a brush with long bristles and in his left, a pointed instrument which has been identified in a variety of ways, one of which is as a pointed stick (of charcoal or lead) with which the artist makes a preliminary sketch on the unfired clay body of the vase.

There have been several suggestions as to the identity of the instruments with which the Attic relief line was produced. Some suggestions have been a brush, a single long bristle, a feather, a reed, a metal pen, and the equivalent of a modern drafting pen made from a quill. Heavy black glaze matter with sufficient consistency to stand up and form a three-dimensional line must be used. When the line dries it must retain its three-dimensional character and still adhere to the body of the vase, and it must survive the firing operation. The tool for producing the line has to be capable of drawing a long line without a break, in some instances well over 6 inches in length. The quantity of matter needed to achieve a continuous 6-inch relief line is considerable. The line, short or long, straight or curved, must be reasonably uniform from beginning to end and should not vary appreciably in width or thickness. It has

207 Detail of a kylix, in the manner of the Antiphon Painter, which shows a vase-painter holding a brush and relief line instrument.

to be capable of being applied delicately enough to render eyes, nostrils, details of lips, teeth, etc., and it must also be able to be turned easily without smearing or changing in width. In my experiments, the instruments mentioned above did not meet these requirements. When the glaze matter was heavy enough to form the proper relief line, it would not flow from the instruments. In addition, many of them, like brushes which are drawn along the surface, could not be used to make the abrupt turns necessary to duplicate the ancient effects.[14]

A relief line similar to the ancient relief line can be produced by extruding or trailing the glaze from a small syringe in much the same way that a pastry chef decorates a cake by extruding the frosting from a pastry tube. In experiments, I used a small metal syringe, similar to a hypodermic syringe, on which I fitted a variety of drawn glass nozzles in order to regulate the

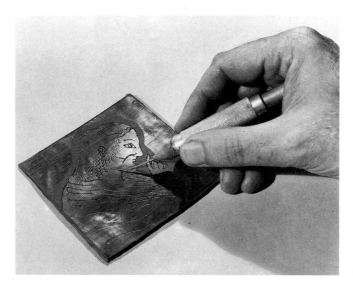

208 *Drawing relief lines with a syringe.*

208   thickness of the extruded line. A line produced in this way occasionally dried with a slight trough, or long ridge, very much like those which sometimes occur in the Attic relief lines. When fired, the line adheres to the body of the vase with great tenacity. If the line is subsequently mechanically broken, it takes with it a part of the clay body and leaves a groove in the vase; the same can be found on ancient vases.

    The drawing instrument used by the Attic vase-painters was probably composed of a tapered nozzle made of bronze, bone, or ivory pierced with a
209   very fine hole. To this nozzle a short piece of animal intestine filled with the heavy viscous glaze matter must have been attached. The end of the intestine section, away from the nozzle, would have been tied so that it could easily be opened in order to add glaze matter as needed. The nozzle would have been held by the vase-painter in his fingers, with the intestine tube section in the palm of the hand. The other fingers would have been used to press against this tube gently so as to force the extrusion of the glaze as required. I believe that
207   the object held in the left hand of the vase-painter shown on the Boston kylix may be a representation of such a drawing instrument.

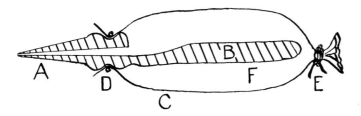

209 *Proposed Attic relief line drawing instrument. A, nozzle; B, nozzle extension for control of instrument; C, collapsible bag; D, bag tied to nozzle; E, opening used to fill bag; F, black glaze matter.*

210 Detail of bell krater fragment, which shows South Italian Apulian relief lines, about 350 BC.

In experiments, the black glaze for the relief line was thickened by allowing it to evaporate longer than the glaze used for the background and decorative elements. To it I added liquid sugar in the form of honey, an old potter's trick to make a glaze stick. An addition of 10% by volume of honey increased the viscosity of the heavy glaze, and permitted it to be extruded properly without drying too rapidly and without spreading on either side of the line on the surface of the vase. The slight amount of salt in the honey also helped to stabilize the line. When the extruded relief line dried, the honey was tacky and adhesive, and prevented the glaze line from flaking off the vase body. The sugar burned away during firing.

The relief line first appeared in Attic black-figured ware of the mid-sixth century BC where it was used sparingly, mostly in ornaments, as for the connecting curved lines between lotus buds, and for the lines separating tongues. It was fully and extensively utilized in Attic red-figured ware, and was particularly effective in the drawing of the human form. The relief line, invented in Attica, found its way to Italy where it was abundantly used. Ill. 210 is an enlarged detail of the hair of Telephos on an Apulian fragment *210* where the extruded appearance is apparent.

211 West Slope ware, third to first century BC.

212 (opposite, above) Jar with applied molded and slip decoration, an example of Roman Barbotine ware, late second century AD. Found at Felixstowe, England, probably from Lezoux, France.

213 (opposite, below) Reproduction of Roman Barbotine ware.

West Slope ware

The use of the relief line made with black glaze continued until the end of the red-figure technique era, in Attica about 320 BC, and in Southern Italy and Etruria a generation later. From the third to the first century BC the relief line technique degenerated with the substitution of a clay slip for the black glaze. Flowers, patterns, or a decorative series of dots were produced using a white or red extruded clay slip, quite often left unglazed to contrast with the black glaze of the balance of the vase. In Attic pottery this ware is known as West
211 Slope ware.

Barbotine ware

By the end of the first century BC the West Slope ware was no longer produced; it was replaced by a coarser type of pottery known as Barbotine in which the extruded relief line was made from clay slip identical to the clay body of the vase. This ware was completely coated with either a black or red glaze. The relief line decorations were often in the form of animals or flower
212 patterns in high relief and were produced with great verve and vitality. Ill. 212 is a Barbotine jar of the second century AD in the British Museum. The decoration has been reproduced on a flat clay slab using the extruded line

214 Chinese false cloisonné ware, AD 1368–1644.

*215 English Staffordshire slipware, seventeenth-eighteenth
century AD.*

technique by Ione Sherman, an amateur potter who was formerly a *213*
professional decorator of pastry cakes. Barbotine ware was manufactured
throughout the entire Roman Empire from the Black Sea to Egypt, Greece,
Italy, Germany, France, and England. It continued until about the fourth
century AD.[15]

False cloisonné ware

The technique of the extruded relief line, which had its origin in Greece in the
mid-sixth century BC, may therefore be traced in modified usage to the fourth
century AD, a span of nine centuries. The relief line technique has been
invented several times independent of former usage. It was used in China
during the Ming Dynasty (AD 1368–1644) to produce a false cloisonné type of *214*
pottery. The vase, made of white clay, was decorated with floral patterns
created by means of a relief line, also done in a white clay. After a preliminary
bisque firing, the looped areas, like the petals of a flower, drawn with the
relief line, were filled with a colored glaze and the vase was fired again. The
relief lines served as tiny walls separating the areas of colored glaze.

Staffordshire slipware

In England, Staffordshire slipware was made in the late seventeenth and early
eighteenth centuries by Thomas, James, Charles, and Ralph Toft. The relief *215*
line was not extruded in the manufacture of this ware, but was produced by
allowing a heavy colored glaze to flow through a small spout at the bottom of
a glaze cup. A vigorous ware was achieved, often depicting human and animal
figures along with patterns and lettering.

Ocher wash

The predominant colors of an Attic vase are the black glaze and the red clay
body, but the Greeks made use of a limited range of additional colors. One of
these was an ocher wash used to heighten the color of the clay body. Attic clay
by itself fires to a yellow-brownish-red, but the vase-painters apparently
wished to have a background of a richer, more contrasting color. I found that
yellow ocher mixed in a thin solution with water duplicated the effect. In
order to have the ocher wash adhere smoothly to the clay body it was
desirable to add an emulsifier, like soap, to the solution. Water, in which
wood ashes have been soaked, is also satisfactory and could have been used in
ancient times. This is similar to the peptizing agent discussed previously.

216 Burnishing an unglazed skyphos.

The ocher wash used by different vase-painters varied considerably. On some vases it is hardly visible; on others it has a strong orange color; sometimes it is powdery; and occasionally it has a shine on its surface. It is hard to judge the original appearance because the ocher coating is soft and can be abraded and leached away by the action of water in the ground. When the ocher wash has a shiny surface, it was probably made by mixing a slight amount of dilute black glaze matter with it. Not too much dilute glaze could be used because interior body lines painted with dilute glaze, as described later, would be invisible. The ocher was applied with a brush, usually over the entire vase as it rotated on a wheel. Circular bands can sometimes be seen.

The underside of the foot was not coated on most vases, and occasionally the neck was left untouched.

The nomenclature for ocher is confusing both as to the ancient names and the modern ones. Ocher is a natural red oxide of iron usually occurring in small lumps which can be easily ground and powdered. The ancient Greeks classified the miltos, or ruddle, by grades of different quality or color and referred to the ocher by the name of its source, Carthaea (Ceos), Lemnos, and Sinope. In the fourth century BC the Athenians and the people of Carthaea renewed an old treaty granting to the Athenians exclusive rights to the famous "red earth," or miltos, of the island.[16] Apparently this was done to insure an uninterrupted supply which was essential for the pottery industry. Today ocher is sold under varying names indicating increasing intensity of the color of the pigment; yellow ocher, red ocher, and "Indian" red.[17]

Burnishing and polishing

It is very important to burnish and polish the surface of the leather-hard clay vessel before the application of the yellow ocher. A rounded agate pebble or a piece of bone or hard wood may be used to smooth and consolidate the surface. A very thin application of yellow ocher is applied with a wide brush and when it has dried, the surface is again burnished or polished. The burnishing of an unglazed skyphos is illustrated on a kylix in Berlin. The iron *216* oxide in the ocher polishes to a very high luster; this is an essential step in yielding the final high quality lustrous black glaze. After the black glaze matter has been applied over the burnished ocher wash, and the black relief lines have been added, it is desirable to polish the whole vase with a soft cloth before firing. This increases the luster of the black glaze, both in the solid areas and in the relief lines.

Dilute glaze

The brown translucent line with which the Attic red-figure vase-painters drew muscles, hair, and other markings as well as shading, is produced by diluting with water the black glaze matter used for the backgrounds. This thin brownish glaze is very easy to use with a small brush. It is therefore perfectly proper to refer to this color, as Beazley and others have done, as dilute glaze. The diluted black glaze matter particles of iron oxide are separated from each other and do not sinter during firing, therefore, they reoxidize to red ferric oxide and yield a brownish tone. The same dilute brown glaze was also used as an outline or to tone an area on certain types of white-ground lekythoi.

Added white

The color scheme of Attic black-figured vases calls for the addition of a white color for women's flesh, shield devices, clothes, furniture, and the like. Some of this white has survived to the present time, but it has often flaked or rubbed off and the only trace we have of it is the dulled area of the black glaze over which the white had originally been painted. This white was produced from a very fine white clay, which was a primary clay and had only a very slight admixture of iron so it fired a relatively pure white with only a faint tone of yellow derived from the iron. The Greeks later refined this clay still further by sedimentation, thus controlling the yellowish cast, or they found a pure white clay source. I was able to duplicate this added white by using native American pipe clay, but the results were too white so that it was necessary to tone the clay with an addition of a scant quantity of red Attic clay.

The added white was applied with a brush, usually over the black glaze, although sometimes directly on the clay body. Where it flakes off after firing, the black glaze underneath shows the dull surface characteristic of Attic black-figure. The same white slip was used on white-ground lekythoi, and occasionally on other vases, and was applied with a brush while the vase rotated on a wheel. The surface could be burnished to a glossy white or left a matte white. This white-ground was an excellent drawing surface for both *v* the black glaze and the dilute brown glaze line.[18]

Yellow

Occasionally added yellow was used, particularly on black-figured skyphoi.[19] It is not a bright true yellow but instead is a beige or ivory tone distinctly different from added white. Both added yellow and added white have appeared on vases at the same time. The added yellow can be made by adding 25% black glaze matter to the white slip. One would expect that the mixture would fire to a light gray shade but it assumes a slightly golden yellow tone.

Gray

If the percentage of black glaze is increased to 75–90% when mixed with white slip, a gray hue does appear. This color was used in ancient times, as reported by Dietrich von Bothmer in *Amazons in Greek Art*: "Another differentiation between the two Amazons is unique, and as far as I can see without parallel in Attic black-figure: the flesh of the dead Amazon is not white like that of her companion but an off-colour of grey – an unexpected touch of realism."[20]

I Attic black-figured amphora by Exekias, c. 540 BC, showing a marriage
procession perhaps of Herakles and Hebe. Ht 18½ in.

II Attic red-figured calyx krater signed by the potter Euxitheos and the painter
Euphronios, c. 515 BC. It depicts Sarpedon, dead, carried by Thanatos and
Hypnos. Ht 18 in.

III Etruscan Caeretan hydria, by the Painter of Caeretan vases, c. 525 BC.
Ht 17⅝ in.

IV Apulian red-figured column krater, attributed to the Group of Boston 00.348, c. 370–360 BC. It shows an artist painting a statue of Herakles. Ht 20¼ in.

V Attic white-ground kylix, by the Villa Giulia Painter, c. 470 BC, showing a woman with scepter and libation bowl. Ht 2½ in.; diam. 8½ in.

VI Attic black-glazed and gilded kantharos, fourth century BC. Ht 8 in.

VII Attic red-figured volute krater with intentional red glaze, by the school of the Kleophrades Painter, c. 480–470 BC. Ht (to tops of volutes) 22¾ in.

VIII Attic red-figured pelike with unfired colors, by the Marsyas Painter, mid-fourth century BC. Ht 17¾ in.

IX Modern reproductions of Attic pottery. Upper pair copied from an Attic black-figured amphora by the Goltyr Painter. Left, unfired. Right, fired. Lower pair copied from an Attic red-figured kylix by the Villa Giulia Painter. Left, unfired. Right, fired.

X Attic black-figured amphora with red misfired spot, by the Rycroft Painter, c. 530–520 BC. Ht 15 in.; diam. 10⅟₁₆ in.

XI Attic red-figured kylix by Douris (potting attributed to Python), c. 480 BC, repaired with the fragment of another kylix.

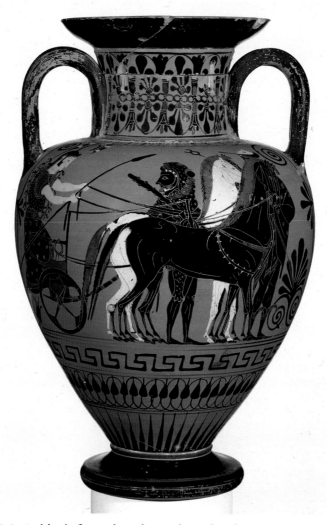

XII Attic black-figured neck-amphora by the Bareiss Painter, c. 520–510 BC, repaired with the mouth of another amphora. Ht 13 in.

Added red

The other principal added color in black-figured vases was the added red used for men's beards, clothes, wreaths, fillets, sashes, blood, shield devices, eyes, inscriptions, etc. This is a red oxide of iron pigment which is mixed with water and 10% black glaze matter as a binder. Applied with a brush, it is normally put over the black glaze. In its use for the tongue pattern on the neck of vases, or for spears and the like, the added red is applied directly on the clay body. It holds better on the black glaze than the white slip and does not flake readily. It does not hold so well on clay ground, nor on top of white, and white was never put over it. Black and brown glaze lines are sometimes drawn on it. The red was used as a matte color in decorating white-ground lekythoi, both for outlines and as a solid tone for costumes.

Pink

Pink was occasionally employed; this was produced by mixing 25% added red in white slip.

Gold

In some Attic vases gold was used to add tone and luster to the drawing. Gold leaf rather than mercury gilding was used. The gold leaf was applied on top of a relief drawing produced by extruding a plain clay slip from the same type of drawing syringe, and it was used to create wings for Erotes, wreaths, *123,217,VI* garlands, necklaces, scepters, kerykeia, and the like.[21]

The extruded clay relief form when dry is coated with white of egg to attach the thin gold leaf. The gold leaf is then pressed into place by means of a brush. A small pointed instrument is used to burnish the gold to the dry clay and the excess gold leaf is cut off and removed. It has been said that the gold leaf could not withstand the firing and therefore was applied to the vase after the firing, but this is not so.[22] The vases were fired below 945°C. whereas the melting point of the gold is 1062°C. The gold leaf used in my experiments withstood the firing cycle and reproduced the gilded effect found on Attic vases. When unfired colors were used the gold leaf could have been applied at the same time.

Intentional red glaze

A special type of color was the sixth- and fifth-century BC intentional red glaze. It was mainly used for zones on kylikes. This was successfully

217 *Detail of chous in the Kerch style, showing extruded clay relief lines and gold leaf. Mid-fourth century* BC.

218 Detail of amphora, by the Kleophrades Painter, showing extruded relief lines and dots. Early fifth century BC.

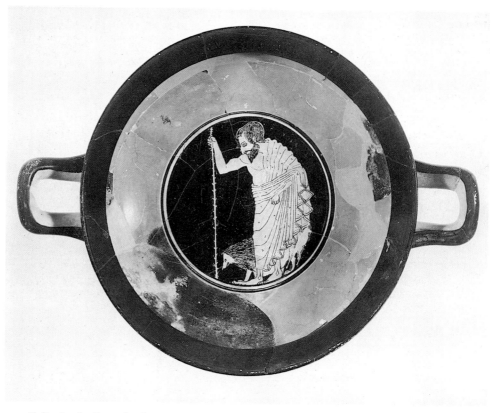

219 *Kylix, by the Hegesiboulos Painter. The area between the tondo and the black band at the lip is of intentional red glaze.*

reproduced by Marie Farnsworth and Harriet Wiseley.[23] In their experiments ocher was added to black glaze matter with a high sintering point so that the mixture turned red during the reoxidizing firing while preserving the shiny surface quality of the glaze. At the same time, adjoining areas in the conventional black glaze with a low sintering point remained black. Apparently, the glaze containing ocher remains porous enough to reoxidize to red whereas the surrounding black areas are more compact and cannot be reoxidized at the same temperature.

219, VII

The intentional red was hard to control in firing, as evidenced by many failures, and it flaked readily owing to its inability to adhere well to the clay body. As a result, it was soon abandoned.

Unfired colors

All of the foregoing ancient colors underwent firing and were accomplished in a single firing cycle. They provided, however, a fairly limited palette.

Certain additional colors were occasionally used which were not fired in the kiln. These fairly fugitive mineral or vegetable colors were painted after firing on some Attic white-ground lekythoi. They included shades of blue, green, yellow, pink, purple, and matte black.[24] Today they are often either completely absent or have faded on vases, the action of sunlight, water in the soil, or burning on a funeral pyre probably having removed them. Dietrich von Bothmer has informed me of a circumstance which proves that they were never fired in a kiln. Certain fragments were subjected to an oxidizing temperature of about 950°C. and the matte black pattern in the border of a white lekythos completely disappeared. The former presence of some of these fugitive colors can be detected by the dull empty square areas left in the meander pattern on some white-ground lekythoi. Occasionally figures appear naked, while in the original state of the vase they were clothed. A

220, VIII

220 Detail of a lekythos, by the Vouni Painter, painted with unfired colors.

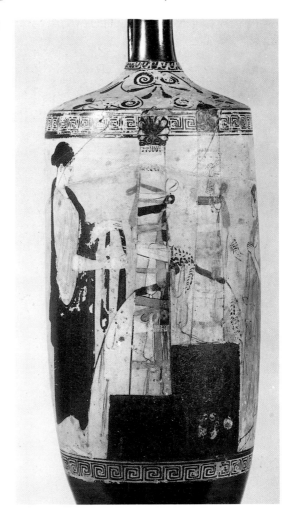

white-ground lekythos which has been burned on a funeral pyre is dull gray in color. Burned vases, however, are sometimes refired in an oxidizing atmosphere by dealers and in museums to restore the original appearance. This is quite successful save that nothing can bring back the missing fugitive colors.[25]

Incision

The incised line which was extensively used in black-figure style was made before firing by the use of a pointed instrument. It was important that the clay body of the vase contained just the proper amount of moisture. If the vase was too damp, the incising tool ploughed in too deeply, creating a furrow. If the vase was too dry, the incising flaked off the dry glaze matter along the edge. As explained above, it was customary to apply the added white over the black glaze. When the incision was made through the white slip, care had to be taken so that the point penetrated the applied white and just faintly scratched the black glaze underneath. In this way, the lines incised in the added white clearly revealed a black layer at the bottom of each groove. The results had a greater contrast and clarity than when the incision accidentally penetrated both layers and revealed the red clay underneath.

Incision was basically a black-figure technique, but it was also used in early red-figure. Whenever a black area such as hair bordered on another black area such as the background, an incised line separated them. Later the delineation was achieved by leaving an unglazed or reserved strip to outline the area. Occasionally the separation for hair was achieved by the use of black glaze extruded to create patterns of dots, as was used to render the hair of 218 Herakles in ill. 218.

Six's technique

Six's technique of East Greek origin, was usually employed on small vases such as lekythoi, phialai, skyphoi, and Nicosthenic amphorae. It made use of the added white, pink, and red. In this technique the picture was painted with a brush, applying the color to the surface of the vase which had been coated with the black glaze matter, and sometimes details or other figures were added by incision. The vase was then subjected to the usual Attic three-stage firing. This was an interesting technique; the pottery is attractive and has a spontaneous quality, but it is somewhat crude, lacking the refinement of the 221 conventional black-figure or red-figure work.

221 *Lekythos decorated in Six's technique (added color and incision).*

223 *Oinochoe, by the Painter of London B620, showing relief appliqué.*

222 *Two-handled cup with stamped decoration.*

224 *Squat lekythos, with relief appliqué.*

Stamped decoration

222 A late Attic technique was the decoration of plain black glazed pottery with designs stamped or impressed in the surface.[26] The vase was allowed to dry slightly after it was formed. While the clay was still fairly soft, lines were impressed in it, and stamps were used to create patterns. A series of dots in a line, often with a progression in the spacing, was not produced by the use of a toothed wheel or roulette as was previously believed, but by a vibrating flexible hooked stick. As the unfired vase rotated on the potter's wheel this chattering tool impressed the series of dots on the surface. Occasionally mold-made appliqués were attached. It was then coated with the black glaze material. This ware imitated metal repoussé vases; many of the stamps apparently were impressions taken from metal originals.[27]

Relief appliqué

Relief appliqués were used in Attic pottery in both the black-figure and the red-figure periods, but never extensively. They were produced by pressing soft clay into a mold in a manner similar to the production of the plastic vases, and then while the molded clay was still moist, it was applied to the moist

223 unfired vase using clay slip as a bonding agent. In ill. 223 the appliqué of a woman's head had been applied at the point of juncture of a handle on a white-ground black-figured oinochoe. The relief molded scene decorating a late squat lekythos was molded, and applied to the vase before the black glaze

224 and the decorative patterns were added.[28]

Modeled element

Other techniques that have been widely used by potters in various parts of the world were only occasionally employed by the Greeks. One of these seldom-used methods was the freehand modeling of design elements such as snakes

225 which were then applied to some geometric-style vases. At the points of attachment of handles, clay lumps were sometimes affixed in imitation of the rivets used in metal vases.

Carved technique

Another technique was the cutting or carving of a vase before firing to create patterns. Open-work cutting was used in the Geometric period mostly for

226 bases. Some Attic vases, usually completely covered with black glaze, were
227 carved with fluting or ribs in imitation of repoussé metal vases. A v-shaped

225 *Amphora, Late Geometric period (c. 700 BC), with modeled elements.*

226 *Stand with openwork base (using carved technique), Geometric period, eighth century BC.*

227 *Hydria carved with ribs (in imitation of repoussé metal vases).*

graver was used to remove the clay from the grooves between the ribs. This was done freehand in order to achieve a tapered form for each rib. Small ribbed vases, such as cups and amphoriskoi, required a minimum of carving, since the effect was achieved primarily by impressing the lines into the surface. An examination of the interior of these vases shows the indented ribs.

Inscriptions

Inscriptions were considered part of the decoration of the vases. Sometimes they were the names of the figures drawn on the vase, or a description of the scene, or a remark. Occasionally inscriptions were addressed to the person using the vase, or gave popular names and salutations. Other inscriptions gave the name of the potter and vase-painter. Some inscriptions were apparently meaningless, and are a series of unrelated letters, often poorly painted. Even a series of dots was sometimes substituted for an inscription. These puzzling practices were done for the sake of design, perhaps to fill an area the artist felt should have an inscription, although he had nothing specific in mind, or he may have been illiterate.[29]

Most inscriptions were painted with a fine brush using black glaze, added red slip, or white slip. If the black glaze was diluted, the letters appeared as a golden brown. Other inscriptions were incised with a fine point in the black glaze of the vase, some before and others after firing.

Two types of inscriptions appear on the under surface of the feet of vases. If the inscriptions were painted they are known as *dipinti*, and were painted before firing. The black glaze, or dilute glaze, was rarely used; most often the *dipinto* was painted with a light red ocher wash and appears as a faint pink color. The ocher wash does not adhere well and sometimes very little of it remains. A *dipinto* usually is only a single or a double letter or some type of a mark. The purpose is not clear, but as they were added by the vase-painter or potter, they may have had something to do with an order by a purchaser.

Incisions, or *graffiti*, were scratched into the clay of the foot usually after firing. Examination under low magnification will reveal the characteristic jagged line of the incision cut into the fired clay. Before firing, the clay was soft, allowing a tool to cut a deep, smooth incision. Again, code marks and single letters are prevalent; however, price information and words are sometimes engraved. It is possible that a *graffito* may have been added by the owner to identify his property, by a trader as a notation of an order or a price, or as a dedication of the vase at a shrine or tomb. Some Attic vases bear Etruscan *graffiti* which are evidence of the extent to which Attic wares were exported.

Reproductions

Color plate IX shows samples I have reproduced both in the black-figure and *IX*
in the red-figure technique. In each case, duplicate specimens show pieces
before and after firing. The upper pair is copied from a figure on an Attic
black-figured amphora by the Goltyr Painter and shows the black-figure *228*
brush painted technique, together with added white and added red, both done
with a brush, and the incision made with a sharp metal point. The lower pair
is copied, using the extruded relief line technique, from the tondo of a red-
figured kylix by the Villa Giulia Painter, and shows the background tone *229*
applied with a brush and the relief line extruded by means of the drawing
instrument. The white fillet and the body muscle lines of dilute brown glaze
were added with a brush.

228 *Detail of black-figured amphora by
the Goltyr Painter. See pl. IX.*

229 *Detail of red-figured kylix by the Villa
Giulia Painter. See pl. IX.*

Chapter Four

FIRING THE VASES

THE TECHNIQUE OF treating dried clay with heat to change it from a soft friable substance to a hard vitreous useful material was discovered by man about 7,000 years ago at the beginning of the Pottery Neolithic period. The discovery was probably accidental, possibly as a result of building a campfire over a deposit of clay. When the fire burned itself out, it was noticed that the clay underneath had become extremely hard. The inventive first potter must have repeated the phenomenon by shaping something from the soft clay and placing it in the fire. When this piece emerged from the firing intact and in a hard permanent form, an industry was born.

The early potters did not use a kiln; they arranged their dried clay vessels in a small pile and then covered them with whatever fuel was available, like wood, charcoal, twigs, straw, or dried dung. Primitive groups in Africa and in both North and South America have continued this particular practice to the present day. This type of firing of course produces uneven results and causes the loss of a substantial number of pots by breakage. The temperature is not uniform in a mound of pots, and some of them do not reach the proper temperature for the vitrification of the clay. Accordingly, when the unvitrified pots have water put in them they dissolve and revert back to soft clay.[1] The color of the pottery is rather unpredictable because some areas of the fire are oxidizing in character and other areas are reducing. Therefore, some of the pottery is a brownish-red in color and some is grayish or black.

Kiln

A kiln is a specially built chamber for firing pottery, which allows the potter more control over the process. Usually there is an area for burning the fuel which is separate from the area in which the pots are located. Openings are provided for tending the fire, for placing and removing the pots, for observing the firing, and for controlling the flow of air through the kiln.

The use of a kiln does not insure the potter of complete success, and a fair number of wasters are produced in each firing. A vivid description of the problems is given in the poem entitled "Kiln" preserved in the pseudo-Herodotean *Life of Homer*.[2] The translation and comments are by Marjorie J. Milne:

If you will pay me for my song, O potters,
then come, Athena, and hold thy hand above the kiln!
May the kotyloi and all the kanastra turn a good black,
may they be well fired and fetch the price asked,
many being sold in the marketplace and many on the roads,
and bring in much money, and may my song be pleasing.
But if you (potters) turn shameless and deceitful,
then do I summon the ravagers of kilns,
both Syntrips (Smasher) and Smaragos (Crasher) and
   Asbetos (Unquenchable) too, and Sabaktes (Shake-to-Pieces)
and Omodamos (Conqueror of the Unbaked), who makes
   much trouble for this craft.
Stamp on stoking tunnel and chambers, and may the whole kiln
be thrown into confusion, while the potters loudly wail.
As grinds a horse's jaw so may the kiln grind
to powder all the pots within it.
[Come, too, daughter of the Sun, Circe of many spells,
cast cruel spells, do evil to them and their handiwork.
Here too let Cheiron lead many Centaurs,
both those that escaped the hands of Herakles and those that perished.
May they hit these pots hard, and may the kiln collapse.
And may the potters wail as they see the mischief.
But I shall rejoice at the sight of their luckless craft.]
And if anyone bends over to look into the spy-hole, may his whole face
be scorched, so that all may learn to deal justly.

This little poem belongs to the category of begging songs, in which demands are made on someone, good wishes for him are expressed, and warning is given of what the singers will do if their demands are not met. Folk songs are especially liable to changes in the text, additions, and so forth, and this has been the case here. The bracketed passage ["Come, too . . . luckless craft"] is later than the rest, probably by several centuries. In the second sentence, the word *kanastra* appears only in a quotation from the poem; the manuscripts have instead two words which do not make sense. *Kanastra* probably belonged to the original text and was replaced, when this type of vase went out of fashion, by another vase name which is corrupt in the manuscripts. The poem itself was apparently taken by Wackernagel to be no earlier than

230 Firing a kiln. See ill. 1.

*c.*430 BC, but this dating is based on an inferior manuscript reading that has unfortunately been adopted by most editors. A precise dating is impossible, but *c.* 520–*c.* 480 BC seems a good guess, though any time between *c.* 520 and *c.* 325 BC would be possible.

Operation

There are a few excellent representations of kilns on Greek pottery. An Attic kiln is shown in ills. 1, 230.[3] The top of it is decorated with a satyr's head to ward off the evils that might befall the pottery during firing. The kiln is stoked by a young fireman while another man approaches with a load of fuel on his shoulders. The proprietor or foreman, an older man, oversees the work while walking about with his staff.

Another kiln being stoked is shown on a Corinthian pinax.[4] During the firing it was very important to regulate the draft, which was done by covering or opening the hole in the top of the kiln. In ill. 232[5] the fireman is shown with a hooked stick with which he will pull a cover over the hole causing the fire to smoke and produce a reducing condition in the kiln.[6] A larger kiln is shown in ill. 233,[7] and the potter has to use a ladder to reach the vent. Ill. 234[8] shows a fragment of a pinax with a closer view of a potter tending the kiln. He carries his hooded stick in his right hand and has climbed up on the kiln to regulate the flame which is shooting out of the vent hole. In ill. 235,[9] the kiln tender is

1,230

231

232

233,234

235

231 *Stoking the kiln.*

232 *Potter climbing on a kiln to close the vent hole.*

233 *Potter mounting a ladder to close the vent hole
of a large kiln.*

234 *Potter using hooked stick to close the vent hole.*

235 *Kiln being fired under reducing conditions.*

236 *Shaking up the fire for the reoxidizing phase.*

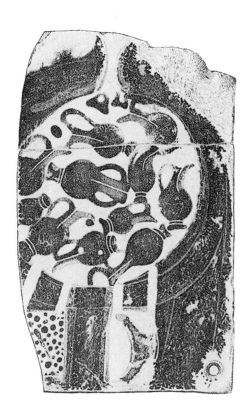

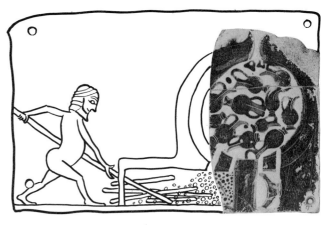

237,238 *Fragment of a pinax, found in 1879 at Penteskouphia near Corinth, showing a schematic diagram of the interior of a kiln; (above) reconstruction of this pinax.*

shown standing on part of a large kiln. Long sticks of wood protrude from the fire box as the door is ajar allowing flames to escape. The door to the pottery chamber of the kiln is visible at the left. It is closed, as is the spy-hole in the door. Apparently the potter has closed the vent hole at the top of the kiln. The

236 fireman in ill. 236[10] is shaking up the fire for the final reoxidizing phase. Flames can be seen spurting out of the top vent hole indicating that an oxidizing condition exists in the kiln.

A schematic diagram of the interior of a kiln is shown on a fragment of

237 another pinax.[11] Less than half of the plaque is preserved; the scene extended to the left and probably showed the stoking tunnel and a potter tending the fire, as proposed by R. M. Cook.[12] The general appearance of the scene

231 would have been similar to the pinax in ill. 231. On that basis, a conjectural

238 restoration is given in ill. 238. In the part of the pinax that is preserved, the vases are shown inside the kiln chamber, which is isolated from the firing by a perforated floor. The burning embers are represented by the dots in the lower left hand corner of the scene. Vases would have been nested and carefully stacked in an actual firing, but here the artist has spread them out to show their shapes. At the bottom right of the pinax is shown a boat-shaped vessel which may have contained water to help the reduction firing. Between it and the embers is a pillar which supported the perforated kiln floor.[13] At the top of the kiln is the vent hole, or chimney, which was covered during the reduction

stage of the firing, and left open during the two oxidizing phases. The vase-painter did not draw the door of the kiln through which the pottery was loaded, nor the small spy-hole in the door or kiln wall which was used to observe the progress of the firing. The two test pieces, which the artist has shown near the vent at the top of the kiln in his idealized depiction of the kiln interior, would have been immediately inside the spy-hole. These two draw pieces were removed one at a time during the course of the firing to test the temperature and the condition of the black glaze. They have holes in them to facilitate their removal with a hooked stick.[14]

Test pieces

Test pieces were unfired clay specimens coated with black glaze. Apparently special test pieces did not have to be made as there was always a surplus of unfired vases that had been broken during decorating. Fragments of these broken vases, sometimes with a hole roughly drilled in them, were used to test the different stages of the three-phase firing cycle. An excellent pair of such test pieces was found in the Athenian Agora.[15] They are fragments of an 239,240 unfinished red-figured bell krater apparently broken during decorating. A hole is preserved in the larger piece. They were withdrawn from the kiln at different times. The larger piece was removed first because it is underfired with a brownish color ranging to black in parts. The smaller fragmentary piece was removed later; it was correctly fired.

239,240 Interior and exterior of some red-figured bell krater fragments, used as test pieces for the different stages of the firing cycle.

Temperature

Contemporary potters use either pyrometric cones with various melting points to help gauge temperatures, or a pyrometer, an electrical temperature recording device, can be installed in the kiln. By observing the bending or sagging of the test pyrometric cones through a spy-hole in the kiln, or by simply reading the dial of the pyrometer, the potter is kept well informed of the temperature of the kiln. The suggestion has been made by Oliver S. Tonks that the ancient Attic potter may have used the equivalent of the pyrometric cones in the form of gold and silver wire in his kiln to ascertain his proper temperatures.[16] The melting points of both gold (1062°C.) and silver (961°C.) are slightly above the temperatures at which ancient potters fired, so this idea is not valid. An alloy of silver could be made which would melt at the correct temperature, but such a device is not necessary. An experienced potter can rely on observations of the various incandescent colors in the kiln to determine the proper temperature. It is relatively easy without cones or instruments to judge the correct temperature for a step in this process within a margin of plus or minus 25°C.[17]

There are no written records of the temperatures used in firing by the ancient Attic potters. To check the maximum temperature at which the ancient black glaze was fired, a test was made based on the work of Charles F. Binns.[18] A fifth-century BC black glazed fragment from Athens was broken into four smaller pieces. Three of these pieces were subjected to different temperatures under oxidizing conditions to determine the maximum temperature at which the black glaze would remain unchanged. The fourth fragment was retained without refiring as a control specimen. It was found that at 945°C. there was no visible change, at 1000°C. the black glaze developed a slightly silvery iridescent appearance, and at 1050°C. the black glaze reoxidized and turned red.[19] Additional tests with modern Attic clay were made. At 825°C. under oxidizing conditions the clay fired merely to a brownish red. At 945°C. it fired to a satisfactory red very similar to ancient Attic pottery. At 1005°C. the red in the clay became more intense and was no longer satisfactory. These tests showed that the highest temperature to which the ancient pottery was subjected could not have been much in excess of about 950°C.

It is to be noted that a wide variation is found in the color of the fired Attic clay, ranging from a gray buff through pink to a reddish orange color. This variation is normal and results from variations in firing temperatures and conditions. Basically the higher the temperature at which the pottery was fired the brighter and more intense would be the reddish color. This is the result of increasing oxidation of the ferric oxide in the clay. If there was a lack of oxygen in the kiln, the color became modified and gray, despite the temperature. The lack of oxygen would have produced partial reducing conditions and inhibited the creation of red ferric oxide. As a consequence, some of the black ferrous oxide remained in the clay. The color of the Attic clay body was controlled by both the temperature and the amount of oxygen in the kiln. Therefore, it is not possible to determine accurately the temperature of the firing merely by observing the color of the fired clay body.

Modern black glaze matter was used to determine the minimum temperature at which the glaze could be formed. A series of tests were made at different temperatures; at over 800°C. the black glaze could be produced, but below that temperature the resulting glaze was red. Apparently the glaze layer does not sinter below 800°C., and the glaze reoxidizes to red ferric oxide. Attic pottery, therefore, was fired at temperatures between 800° and 950°C.[20]

Stacking

In firing the vases, the ancient Greeks used a kiln heated by wood or twigs. The thoroughly dry pottery, coated with the glaze matter, was placed in the kiln and, as the black glaze did not melt in the firing process, it was possible to stack one piece on top of another without the vases sticking to each other. The ancient potters stacked their vases by nesting kylikes in skyphoi or in other kylikes and smaller pots in larger ones, which is unlike current ceramic practice. The contemporary potter uses glazes which contain a higher percentage of silica that fuse during the firing operation and form a glassy surface very susceptible to damage during the firing. Consequently, the contemporary potter is forced to separate his glazed pieces by either not glazing the bottom of his pots, or by placing them on small clay stilts. It is common modern practice to fire pots unpainted and, when they are in a completely hard vitrified state, to decorate or glaze, and then refire them.

Firing cycle

The ancient Attic potters used only one firing cycle. To fire the black glaze in the manner of ancient potters, heat is applied to the kiln and the temperature is increased under oxidizing conditions. This is automatic in an electric kiln, but in a kiln fired by wood or twigs, firing is accomplished by allowing free access of air to the kiln. When the temperature reaches 800°C. the atmospheric condition is changed to that of a reducing atmosphere. In an electric kiln this is achieved by the introduction of a handful of wet sawdust which simulates the green wood probably used by the ancient Attic potter. In a wood-fired kiln, the air vents should be closed and a large quantity of green wood, which produces smoke, should be thrown into the fire box. It is important that this reducing atmosphere be maintained for not less than a half hour by the addition of the wet sawdust or green wood. Potters call this phase a "soaking" period. The temperature is increased gradually, still maintaining the reducing atmosphere, until 945°C. is reached. Then, while continuing to maintain the reducing atmosphere, the temperature is allowed to decrease slowly to about 900°C. At this point the last of the wet sawdust or green wood is consumed, and a small amount of fresh air is introduced by opening an air hole in the kiln. This changes the atmosphere from reducing to oxidizing. The kiln is slowly cooled to room temperature maintaining the oxidizing atmosphere, at which point the vase, with its characteristic red and black colors, is finished. The chemistry of the changes in color of the glaze during firing is discussed in Chapter Two. Reduction firing is sometimes practiced by modern Asiatic, European, and American potters, who attempt to create random variations in surface colors, but such patterns are created largely by chance, and are not under the direct control of the potter.

Occasionally in fragments of Attic and South Italian pottery evidence can be found of the three-step firing cycle. This is indicated by the grayish tone of part of the clay as seen in a fracture. This grayish color occurs away from the glazed edge of the fragment and is best seen in the center of a broken stem of a kylix where the clay is quite thick. The gray color indicates that this center area did not completely reoxidize in the third stage of the firing. Spectrographic analyses of the gray area and the adjacent red areas show them to be identical in elements present.

Shrinkage and weight loss

During firing, Attic clay shrinks and loses weight; as the temperature increases these effects become more pronounced. They can be minimized by adding sand or crushed rock to the clay as a temper. Shrinkage and weight loss were discussed in Chapter One and are recorded in Graph I (shrinkage of Attic clay) and Graph II (loss of weight of Attic clay). The average shrinkage of Attic vases at 945°C. was $9\frac{1}{2}$% with a 33% loss of weight.

An examination of Graph I shows a marked shrinkage between 1000°C. and 1050°C. Higher temperatures cause increased shrinkage, softening, and warpage of the clay. This almost never happened in an ancient firing, but it did occur frequently when vases were placed on funeral pyres, or were

241

241 Warped fragments from a funeral pyre, part of a white-ground lekythos, by the Painter of the Group of the New York Hypnos.

subjected to accidents or to the destruction of a city by fire. The intense heat in such situations caused them to crack and warp. Sometimes the black glaze was destroyed by reoxidizing it to red. On other occasions vases in smoky pyres were reduced by the lack of oxygen; they were also carbon smudged and the red clay emerged colored an unattractive gray. Refiring such a vase in an oxidizing atmosphere to a temperature of 850°C. restores the red color to the clay, but if the heat has caused warpage nothing can be done to restore the shape.

An increase in temperature also results in an increase in the hardness of the fired clay, as recorded in Graph III (hardness of fired Attic clay). The increase is quite consistent over the temperature span of 615°C. to 1050°C. which exceeds the range used in making Attic pottery.

Accidents

Accidents frequently destroyed pottery in the kiln. An air bubble which had not been removed by proper wedging of the clay of a single vase could have expanded during firing and burst the vase, causing those stacked above it to collapse in a broken heap. Incomplete drying could cause the same result because the moisture in the clay would have turned to steam and shattered the pottery. A study of the minor mishaps which have occurred in the production of Attic vases is very enlightening.[21] The large red areas which are considered defects on many Attic vases were caused by several different conditions. The presence of a draft in the kiln might cause a cool area on the vase and prevent it from reaching the sintering temperature necessary for the formation of a

242 permanent black oxide. A similar result will occur if one part of the kiln is cooler than another. Then the side of the vase that has not reached the sintering temperature will remain red. Added white or red colors applied over black glaze will in some borderline cases prevent the glaze from sintering, and it will reoxidize to a red color. This effect is revealed if the added white or red color has flaked off. The other, and rarer, type of brownish area was produced when a section of a vase was overheated in the reoxidizing firing to the point that the black glaze reoxidized and lost its black color. Sometimes this type of area can be recognized by the presence of a slight iridescence over

243 the black glaze on the rest of the vase.

Occasionally, marks were caused on a vase by another vase during the firing process. This most frequently occurred when the temperature in the kiln did not exceed the sintering temperature of the black glaze. Accordingly,

244,245 if a kylix was nested in a skyphos, or a lid was inverted on its bowl, and the

242 *Pelike, by the Westreenan Painter, showing a red streak from too low a firing temperature.*

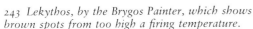

243 *Lekythos, by the Brygos Painter, which shows brown spots from too high a firing temperature.*

244,245 (top) *Misfired interior of bowl caused by protection of an inverted lid, and too low a firing temperature; (above) misfired area of the lid which was inverted on the bowl during firing.*

temperature in the kiln only reached the sintering point for the outside exposed areas of the vases, then the inside areas were prevented from reaching the sintering temperature, and did not turn a permanent black but reoxidized to red. Sometimes only the ring of contact remained red or discolored, or a slight iridescence of the black glaze is the only sign of the contact with the other vase. This effect is not related to the lack of smoke or reducing atmosphere reaching these areas but is a function of temperature.

A puzzling large red circle occurs on the body of some vases, particularly amphorae. Normally an amphora would have been fired standing upright on its foot, but in stacking a kiln the potter tried to utilize all available space. Evidently with a kiln almost full to the roof an amphora might be placed on its side balancing horizontally on the mouth of another amphora. A marginal firing temperature would have caused the red ring of contact.

x

A very fine black glaze will sometimes have a slight bluish cast which is related to the silvery iridescence caused by a dangerously high temperature. This color is due to the interference of light waves that are reflected back and forth within the outermost layers of the glaze. Often a vase having black glaze with a bluish cast will also have a damaged spot due to overheating. At about 1000°C. a very thin surface layer of black glaze oxidizes to red ferric oxide and causes a plane of potential cleavage between it and the unaltered black glaze. This provides the layer which causes the interference effect with light. The silvery iridescent coating can be removed readily by scraping with a sharp blade. Murray Pease demonstrated that the coating could be dissolved with hydrofluoric acid. When the acid is removed from the surface of the vase with a cotton swab, a brownish residue appears on the swab. This is the red ferric oxide layer. When the same test is repeated on normal black glaze, only a gray residue of black ferrous oxide appears on the swab.

In late Attic pottery, particularly in stamped or impressed black ware, the silvery iridescent effect is very prevalent and appears to have been done deliberately. Possibly the effect was thought to cause the vase to appear as if it were made of metal.

A dull brownish gray tone of the glaze resulted from an insufficient reduction period in the firing or a lack of water vapor in the kiln.

246 Pelike, by the Theseus Painter; the streaked red figures were caused by the black glaze being applied too thin, so that the figures reoxidized to red.

247 Kylix, by the Antiphon Painter, which shows figures drawn with one batch of glaze; the background is from a different batch with a higher sintering temperature.

Another variation is a black glaze with a greenish tone. The iron in the Attic black glaze usually was suspended in the colloidal state, but if too much alkali were used in the preparation, the iron dissolved in the glaze and imparted a greenish tint.[22]

A glaze that had been applied too thin would show reddish streaks. Such a thin glaze can readily reoxidize to become a large streaked red area. The vase-painter of the black-figured pelike in ill. 246 painted his figures with a glaze 246 that was too thin. Accordingly the figures reoxidized to red, except in the areas which he went over twice. The outline of the figures, their faces, and the folds of their garments which were painted first have an extra coat of glaze and have remained black.

Another defect sometimes occurred when a vase was painted with glaze matter from two batches having slightly different sintering points. A firing that reached the sintering temperature of one glaze batch but not the other resulted in a vase with well defined red or dull black areas which follow the outline of the drawing. Ill. 247 shows a section of a kylix in which the figures 247 were drawn with a glaze that had a sintering temperature lower than the glaze used to fill the background. The firing temperature was sufficient to cause the "eighth-inch" contour stripe around the figures to turn black but the background remained red.

248 *Detail of an amphora, which shows where the vase was dented by another vase during drying.*

Ghost

A more interesting and rarer defect is a "ghost" image on a vase. A well defined "ghost," first observed by Reichhold, occurs on an Attic red-figured pelike by the Berlin Painter in Vienna which is very accurately described and well illustrated by Fritz Eichler.[23] The image of a face has been transferred from another red-figured vase to this one, and at the location of the transfer the vase is dented. This transfer occurred after the vase was painted and while it was drying. Undoubtedly, when it was placed on a shelf in the drying room, it bumped against an adjoining vase, and the image from one vase was transferred to the other in much the same way as a rubber stamp functions. Naturally, the transferred image is a reverse or "mirror" image.

It has been suggested that this type of "ghost," or more accurately, transfer, and these dents had occurred during firing. This is not the case, for when a vase had been thoroughly dried (as it had to be before being placed in the kiln), it was in a fragile condition. Any blow which could have dented it would have caused its destruction. The temperature in the kiln did not reach the point at which the vase would become soft and malleable as in the making of glassware. An additional proof pointed out by Eichler is the fact that the encircling lines painted in added red, which are on the Vienna pelike, were damaged by the accident, and were touched up by the vase-painter *before* firing.

"Ghosts" often occur on red-figured lekythoi because the tall cylindrical shape of the vase permitted them to be grouped in close proximity. Vases with small bases easily allowed for an accident of one toppling against another. In some instances this caused a slight dent in the vase and also some of the clay *248* from one vase to adhere to the other. This could not occur during firing because the black glaze was not vitreous, and even when a vase was placed in contact with an adjoining black glaze surface in the kiln, they would not melt and adhere to each other. The transfer had to occur during drying when the black glaze was tacky.

An outstanding example of a "ghost" occurs on a red-figured lekythos in *249,250* New York. On it is painted a running woman, while on the back are parts of two separate female figures which are "ghosts" transferred from two other red-figured lekythoi. These transfers occurred when the other two vases touched this one before drying.

249,250 Detail of red-figured lekythos, by the Aischines Painter, showing a woman running. A further detail shows, on the reverse of this vase, two "ghost" images which have been transferred from two other red-figured lekythoi.

251 Detail of a column krater, by the Pig Painter, with a "ghost" image visible in the mouth.

Two other types of "ghosts" occurred during firing, and were caused by the contact of vases during either too low or too high temperatures. If the temperature were near the low borderline, a vase nesting inside another vase might inhibit the glaze from turning black at the point of contact. The glaze pattern on one vase could absorb enough heat so that it would appear as a red "ghost" on the other. This has occurred on a red-figured unframed column *251* krater by the Pig Painter in Cleveland, which was drawn to my attention by Dietrich von Bothmer. The "ghost" appears on the inside of the neck and consists of two vertical bands of decorative border patterns and traces of figures from both sides of a framed panel column krater. On the side illustrated, the "ghost" is reversed both left to right and black to red. The black shapes are the feet of two dancing komasts or satyrs. On the other side, not illustrated, a man in a himation leans on his staff. The vase which produced the "ghosts" also appears to be by the Pig Painter.

A "ghost" produced by contact at too high a temperature is a silvery iridescent color and may be seen, under a strong light, by turning the vase. The iridescent areas correspond to red areas on the other vase. This type of "ghost" can be found on the inside of the neck of wide-mouthed vases and on the flat rims of column kraters.

Spall

A different type of defect which sometimes occurred in Attic pottery is a spall. 252
A spall, or chip, resulted from improper purification of the clay and the inclusion in the vase body of a small pebble of quartz or limestone. During firing, a quartz pebble would expand more than the clay and either cause the vase to break or a conical flake to detach from the surface of the vase. A careful examination of the location of such a flake usually reveals a quartz pebble imbedded in the vase body. Not only does quartz have a different coefficient of expansion than the clay body but also at 573°C. the quartz crystals undergo what is known as the change from alpha to beta quartz. At this point in a rising temperature, quartz will suddenly increase its volume by 2%. Conversely, in a decreasing temperature, it will reduce its volume by 2%. This inversion of quartz was particularly harmful to ancient pottery if the heating or cooling process was performed rapidly. During a slow firing, the ware could withstand this shift of volume of a quartz inclusion.

If limestone were present in the clay during firing, it decomposed to calcium oxide. The process was completed at temperatures over 898°C.; Attic pottery was normally fired slightly higher. The calcium oxide remaining in the clay after firing was hygroscopic, absorbed moisture from the air, and became calcium hydroxide. At the same time, it expanded and caused spalling or cracking of the vase. The fact that this rarely occurred in Attic pottery is proof of the existence of an effective ancient purification process of the clay.

252 Detail of a red-figured pelike, by the Walters Painter, about 470 BC. Note the limestone spall in the border, and the handle reattached with bronze rivets.

Chapter Five

CONCLUSION

THE FOLLOWING IS appended as an outline of the customary steps involved from the clay pit to the finished conventional vase.

Steps in the making of an Attic vase

A Digging the clay from the clay pit.

B Washing the clay and allowing it to settle in large excavated pits used as settling basins to rid it of impurities.

C Allowing the clay to age for a few months and to "ripen" by mixing with it small quantities of older clay to increase bacterial action in the clay and to promote its working qualities.

D Drying the clay to a workable consistency.

E Wedging or working the clay to make it smooth and to eliminate air bubbles.

F Forming the vase.

   1 By potter's wheel:
     a The entire vase is thrown on a potter's wheel, or if it is too large to be formed in one operation, the vase is thrown in a series of sections and the sections are joined by wet clay slip.
     b The vase, in a semi-dry condition, is again placed on the wheel and is turned while the potter uses a sharp tool to remove unwanted clay.
     c The vase is smoothed with a moistened cloth, leather, or sponge.
     d Handles and other adjuncts are attached.

   2 By mold:
   Plastic vases are partially produced on the potter's wheel, i.e., the mouth of the vase; the plastic parts are pressed in molds, and then joined, smoothed, and refined by hand.

G Decorating the vase.

   1 Black-figure technique:
     a Polish vase with burnisher.
     b Apply yellow ocher wash.[1]
     c Polish yellow ocher wash.
     d Preliminary sketch with pointed stick of charcoal or lead.
     e Paint the black-figure contour.
     f Fill in the black-figures.
     g Apply added white.
     h Apply added red.
     i Incise lines.
     j Re-apply black or red on white.
     k Polish with soft cloth.

   2 Red-figure technique:
     a Polish vase with burnisher.
     b Apply yellow ocher wash.
     c Polish yellow ocher wash.
     d Preliminary sketch with pointed stick of charcoal or lead.
     e Outline figures with broad band of glaze using brush ("eighth-inch" stripe).
     f Draw relief lines with drawing instrument.
     g Draw dilute brown lines with thin brush.
     h Fill in background working up to broad outline band.[2]
     i Apply added white or red, or relief form, and gold leaf.
     j Polish with soft cloth.

H Firing

   1 Firing under oxidizing conditions up to 800°C.
   2 Firing under reducing conditions with the addition of water vapor from 800°C. to 945°C., and then cooling to 900°C.
   3 Reoxidization at 900°C.
   4 Gradual cooling of the kiln under reoxidizing conditions before removing the finished vase.

Appendix I

DATING AND LOCALIZATION

THE DATING OF Attic pottery may be undertaken by a variety of methods. The most exact is based on an absolute chronology provided by external evidence. Certain historical dates such as the destruction of the Acropolis by the Persians, the mass burial at Marathon, and the reburial of the contents of graves on Delos on the island of Rheneia provide convenient *terminus ante quem* dates for pottery found in these deposits. While the pottery cannot be later than these dates, it *can* be earlier; therefore, discretion must be used. A relative chronology can be established by the internal evidence which may be observed in the continual developmental evolution of vase shapes and painting. Indeed, the dating of Attic pottery on stylistic grounds can be so accurate that the chronology of a single vase-painter's output may be determined, as has often been demonstrated by Sir John Beazley.[1] Care has to be taken to detect the work of stragglers and archaists.

Carbon 14

Technical methods of dating, however, are now being developed.[2] They are not accurate enough for Attic ware but they are useful for prehistoric pottery. Radiocarbon dating using Carbon 14, which has been successfully employed in other archaeological fields, unfortunately has no direct application to pottery for the simple reason that suitable carbon is not present in it. An indirect method of dating is possible if the pottery is discovered together with burned wood or bone which can be dated. Several other scientific methods now offer considerable promise.

Magnetic

Magnetic dating is based on the principle that iron-bearing clay when fired acquires a minute charge oriented to the earth's magnetic field at the time of the firing. The magnetic field of the earth shifts slowly but perceptibly over the centuries so that the orientation of the present field differs from that of classical times. The measurement of the amount of this difference can be used for dating. This can best be done with fired clay found *in situ*; for example, the floor of an ancient kiln. A sample, carefully marked as to its orientation, is removed and sent to the laboratory for reading. There are many variables in this process, but useful results can be obtained.

To a lesser degree, magnetic dating can be used for a single pot even though it has been moved many times since firing. In one system it is necessary to know the location of the pot's manufacture. Assuming that at the time of firing it stood level on its foot, it would have recorded in its magnetic charge the dip or inclination of the earth's magnetic field, which also changes over the centuries. The variation can be detected, and by means of it a calculation of age can be established.

A different system of magnetic dating is based on the continual decline in the earth's total magnetic force. Today this force has diminished in intensity to approximately half what it was about 2,000 years ago. When clay is fired it preserves in it the intensity of the magnetic field at the time of firing. Accordingly, an ancient vase has a more intense magnetic charge than a modern one. A careful measurement of this minute charge may be used to determine the approximate age of the vessel.

An alternative use of the slight magnetic field of fired clay is the detection of buried kilns by the use of the proton magnetometer. This very sensitive device has been used successfully to locate Romano-British pottery kilns in areas where there were no surface indications of such remains. The kiln floors of clay acquired a substantial magnetic charge from the many firings, and when readings of the area are taken with the proton magnetometer the points of greatest magnetic attraction are detected, revealing the buried kilns.

Thermoluminescent

Another method of technical dating of pottery is the thermoluminescent process. It is based on the fact that all matter, including fired or unfired clay, is damaged by the slight amount of nuclear radiation produced by minute amounts of thorium and uranium present in most rocks. When pottery is fired, the heat erases the radiation damage strain in the clay and the process starts anew in the fired pottery. A sample of the pottery under test is heated to a few hundred degrees Celsius and a minute amount of light is emitted. This is caused by the energy released as the distortions of the crystal structure of the fired clay disappear. The light output is measured and a calculation of age is determined. This system also has many variables and is still in the developmental stage.

Although the thermoluminescent technique is today the best physical method for dating ancient pottery it is subject to a wide margin of error of up to 40–50% for a single vase in an existing collection. If a piece is excavated, and a sample of the soil is recovered for testing, the error may be reduced to 15%. For Attic pottery the main value of this test is to check for possible forgery.

Microscopic

A completely different approach to the problem was taken by F. Oberlies and N. Köppen as part of a general investigation of the ancient black glaze.[3] They made a series of microphotographs of cross-sections of the clay body and black glaze of Mycenaean, Attic geometric, black-figure, red-figure, and South Italian pottery. These photographs revealed an evolution of the black glaze which improved in quality from the Mycenaean to the red-figure period. The specular reflection of the glaze is predicated on the smoothness of the surface and the parallel arrangement of the minute platelets sintered in the glaze. In South Italian pottery the quality declined owing to a deterioration in the technique of the preparation of the glaze, and the fact that the clay was not so fine as Attic. Accordingly, larger platelets are present in the South Italian black glaze than in high quality Attic ware. This technique of examination offers a method of relative dating of pottery and in some cases an indication of the location of production.

Spectrographic analysis for localization

To determine the area of the manufacture of pottery, spectrographic analysis may be used. Basically, the spectrographic analysis of the clay of the vase under study is compared with the analysis of clay from a known site. Unfortunately, this method is not so precise as one would wish because the analyses usually do not match as exactly as do a pair of fingerprints. The differences in adjoining clay pits, different strata in the same pit, and the similarity of structure of clays in a large area, complicate the problem. What, then, can, and what cannot, be expected from this procedure?

A comparison of the composition of the Greek clays, ancient and modern, with non-Greek clays (for example, a fragment of a South Italian Apulian bell krater of about 350 BC, Table I, column 5), reveals many actual differences. Primarily the Apulian clay lacks many of the heavier minerals present in the Greek clays. Column 6 is the analysis of the clay of a fifth-century BC Etruscan fragment which is similar in composition to the Apulian piece. Note that nickel and chromium occur only in the Greek clays.

Table I, columns 2, 3, 4 shows that samples of three clays from Athens, Chalkis, and Aegina are quite similar; vases made from these clays would be indistinguishable from each other. However, concerning the problem of the location of production of Chalcidian pottery, spectrographic analysis is useful. Analyses were made of a Chalcidian hydria and amphora, and they were found to be identical. They were also identical to the sample from Chalkis. They did not resemble any of the South Italian clays thus far analyzed. It cannot be said categorically that the two vases were made in Chalkis because of the similarity of clay from Attica and nearby locations, but the tests do seem to rule out Southern Italy as the place of manufacture as some scholars have suggested. This evidence indicates further study should be undertaken as to a pottery site near Chalkis.

Both the clay body and the black glaze of a Corinthian amphora were analyzed. It was found that, unlike Attic practice, where both the black glaze and the clay body were made from the same clay, the Corinthian black glaze was made from a clay different from that used for the body of the vase. The Corinthian clay is a cream color and not suitable for making black glaze, although there is a substantial amount of iron present in it. The black glaze was made from a clay resembling an Attic clay. It would seem unlikely that the Corinthian potters would go to the trouble of procuring Attic clay to make their black glaze. However, a red clay source was used. Apparently this red clay was obtainable in only limited amounts or had to be transported a considerable distance. For the forming of large numbers of vases a potter must have an ample and handy clay source. The only large and readily accessible Corinthian clay source was of a light cream-colored clay, for when the Corinthian potters attempted to imitate the red and black color scheme of Attic vases, they were forced to make their vases from the cream-colored clay and coat them with a red clay slip.[4]

As the clay body and black glaze of Corinthian pottery were made from two different clays, they had different coefficients of expansion. During firing and cooling, the body and the glaze expanded and contracted at different rates which resulted in a poor bond between the two. This would account for the tendency of the black glaze to flake on Corinthian pottery.

A black-figured amphora attributed by Dietrich von Bothmer to the Hyblaea Class, which was thought to have been Attic ware,[5] was discovered in all probability not to have been made on the Greek mainland. After analyzing the clay body, it was found that the clay content resembled South Italian or Sicilian clay more nearly than Attic pottery. The Hyblaea Class is named from Megara Hyblaea on Sicily where such a vase was found. The appearance of the black glaze is quite dull, unlike the sheen of Attic black glaze. Also, the color of the clay body is paler than Attic ware and the ocher wash, which is somewhat powdery, is unusual in that it has been coated over the underside of the foot. This test has apparently indicated the existence of an early type of South Italian black-figured ware stylistically based on Attic pottery.

There are many archaeological problems to which this method of investigation can profitably be applied. For example, Mycenaean-style pottery has been found at many sites in Greece and in the eastern Mediterranean. How much of this pottery was made at Mycenae? Where else in Greece was it made? What were the other production centers outside of Greece? Can trade routes be determined? Other questions and applications readily come to mind.[6]

The spectrographic method of determining the place of origin of a pottery object could also be applied to stone such as marble and limestone. However, the practice of exporting uncut marble blocks would negate the assumption that a statue positively had been carved near the place of origin of the stone. For the same reason, analyses would be of only limited value in attempting to identify the place of origin of objects made of metals such as bronze, silver, and gold. The metals were constantly being traded, melted down, and reused. Results of such analyses would have to be used with caution.

Neutron activation

A different method of analysis for localization was undertaken by E. V. Sayre and R. W. Dodson.[7] Clay samples and sherds were irradiated in a nuclear reactor and the decay curves of the resulting radioactivity were plotted. The decay curves varied for clays from different sites as the component parts of the clay varied in their susceptibility to become artificially radioactive. This process is now more sensitive than spectrographic analysis, and about fifteen elements in pottery can be measured accurately. This has enabled researchers to determine quite precisely the origin of pottery and the sources of the clays employed.

Temper analysis

Another method of detecting the location of manufacture is the examination of the temper which was added to the clay to give it a stiffer working property, accelerate drying, and to minimize shrinkage. A strong hand lens, or a binocular microscope, can be used to identify the temper, which may be sand, crushed rock, volcanic lava, or a variety of identifiable added substances. Identification can be more exact if microscopic thin sections are prepared and a petrographic microscope is used to determine the angle of polarization and index of refraction of minute crystals. For example, I found that certain pottery from Pylos has beach sand containing crushed shells added to the red clay. This constitutes a rare type of temper which an inland site would not have made possible and therefore identifies the location of the ware as having been made in a coastal town. In addition, it indicates a low firing temperature, because the calcium carbonate of the shells would be destroyed at a high temperature. It is important that the pottery be cleaned before examination, otherwise material clinging to the surface may appear to be mixed with the clay. This is especially noticeable in micaceous soil where the tiny plates of mica adhere to a fractured edge. Dietrich von Bothmer found fragments at Thasos which at first glance appeared to be made from a local micaceous clay. When cleaned, it was evident that they were Attic imports.

In the best Attic ware, temper was not added because it was not needed. The Attic clay had a very fine sand occurring with it in the clay pit which helped give the clay excellent working properties. The absence of added temper helps to identify Attic ware.

A substantial amount of work will have to be done in this field to yield productive results for classical sites, although great strides have been made in applying it to the study of pre-Columbian American pottery.[8] A beginning has been made by Marie Farnsworth who can differentiate between Attic, Corinthian, and Aeginetan samples.[9]

Even the earth incrustation and the condition of the surface of the vase may be of assistance in determining the location of burial. Some earth is benign and some destructive. Vases found in Italy at Nola appear as new with a perfect surface, and many from Spina have a powdery rubbed appearance and lack color.

Forgeries

In order to detect a forgery, it is best to remember that every object made by man carries within it the evidence of the time and place of its manufacture. It is a challenge to the trained eye of the art historian and to the technical examination of the scientific analyst to penetrate beneath the surface appearance and to discover the truth.[10] Within the field of Greek ceramics the techniques now available, including microscopic,[11] ultra-violet,[12] x-ray,[13] spectrographic analysis,[14] and thermoluminescent analysis, if properly applied, can detect any type of forgery. The thermoluminescent test is now the most definitive because it proves either that the vase was fired in antiquity, or recently.

253 Polyxena's broken hydria, by the Painter of the Leagros Group. Compare the cracked krater in ill. 67.

254 *Detail of Panathenaic amphora, by the Antimenes Painter, showing holes drilled to receive rivets of lead or bronze.*

255 *Detail of column krater with ancient rivets.*

Appendix II

CONDITION, REPAIR, AND PHOTOGRAPHY

UNFORTUNATELY, OF THE many vases produced, only relatively few have survived, and even fewer are intact or in the same condition as when they left the kiln. Attic vases were made for daily use or for funeral purposes. Inevitably most were broken, and the fragments were either lost or thrown in *253* wells to filter the water. Some vases, however, were so highly prized that they were mended when broken and put back into use. Holes were drilled along *254* the edges of the fragments to receive rivets of lead or bronze, and when reassembled they were held together with clamps. Sometimes a missing piece *255* in a vase was replaced in restoration with a fragment from a different vase.[1] *XI, XII* Pine pitch was probably applied to the cracks to make them watertight. If a kylix stem was broken, a long bronze rivet was used to unite the foot and the bowl. Some amphorae have been found with a large hole pierced in the base which may have been used for libations at the burial. They were restored immediately afterwards with a small plaque and a rivet in order to keep food for the deceased.[2] South Italian vases which were intended solely for funeral purposes, and which therefore did not have to be practical, were often made with an opening between the body and the foot. Occasionally, they had sections such as feet not only created separately but also fired separately. They were joined to the body of the vase with adhesives such as pine pitch, casein, and asphalt.[3]

Burial

Unlike ancient sculpture, no vase has survived to the present in its former location above ground. Burial may have been accidental or subsequent to military destruction of an area. In most cases it resulted from the interment of useful objects including vases as part of the funeral ceremony; sometimes the vases were used as cinerary urns to hold the ashes of the deceased. The custom was widespread in Greece and was practiced in Southern Italy by the Greek

ARCHAEOPHILORVM . SODALITIO . LONDINENSI.
GVGL.HAMILTONVS.BAL..ORD.EQVES.
D.D.D.

*256 The Etruscans buried with their dead
many Greek vases acquired by trade. This
engraved frontispiece shows Sir William
Hamilton and Emma Hart at the opening of
a tomb at Nola in 1790.*

colonies. The Etruscans also buried with their dead many Greek vases which
had been acquired by trade.

Often, although a vase had been buried intact, it was broken by the collapse
256 of the tomb or by ancient grave robbers searching for jewelry made of
precious metal. In such cases, however, the fragments usually remain together
and therefore can be found and reassembled. The François vase, now in the
Archaeological Museum at Florence, had been smashed by grave robbers,
and its fragments were wantonly scattered over an area equal to that of the
Colosseum in Rome. Alessandro François excavated this area and recovered
most of the pieces of the one vase.

Cremation

At various times, cremation, instead of interment, caused vases filled with oil
to be burned on the funeral pyre. As a result, definite gray or black

discoloration, complete loss of fugitive colors, warpage, and breakage occurred. Although the remains of the pyre might be buried the fragments were often scattered and lost.

Unlike gold and silver, the clay of pottery is not intrinsically valuable, nor can it be melted down and re-used. Neither will it oxidize like iron or bronze. It is impervious to bacterial action, and it will not decay like wood, ivory, leather, and cloth. These facts account for its survival under unfavorable conditions which so often caused the destruction or theft of other objects in tombs.

Ground water

Even though a vase survived intact in a tomb, other mishaps might have befallen it. Earth sifted into the tombs, and ground water infiltrated during the rainy season. The ground water might have carried in suspension lime or silica which would be deposited on the vase as a hard white encrustation. Such a deposit would be increased with time in the same manner as ground water creates cave deposits in the form of stalactites and stalagmites. Sometimes bronze or iron objects in the tombs came into contact with the vases and left an oxidized coating adhering to their surface. The plants and trees growing over an ancient necropolis also contributed to the problem. Their roots sometimes penetrated the tombs, forced apart the roof stones and caused them to collapse. Occasionally, roots entwined around a vase leaving

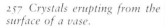
257 Crystals erupting from the surface of a vase.

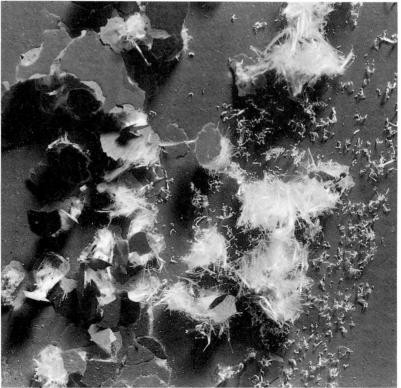

on it a pattern of root marks as organic stains and discolorations. Sometimes the deposits of lime or silica follow the outline of the roots themselves.

Instead of coating the outside of the vase, the water could penetrate the clay body and leave a deposit of salts in the body itself. When such a vase is removed from the ground, the moisture in the air may combine with these salts, causing them to erupt from the surface of the vase as a white powdery coating or as crystalline "whiskers." In some extreme cases, the crystals will push up flakes of the black glaze and destroy the surface of the vase. Occasionally the reverse action occurred. Ground water, permeating the tomb and the vase, would dissolve and leach out of the vase some of the clay body and leave the vase in a porous and weakened condition.

The added colors made of red and white clay slip did not adhere as well as the black glaze and consequently tended to flake off and be lost.

Cleaning

In cleaning a vase, one must differentiate between a recently excavated piece and one that has long stood in an old collection. The latter usually has been exposed to dust, dirt, and grime, and often has a coating of wax which has become discolored. A solution of ammonia will remove most of the grease and dirt, and the incisions may be cleaned out with a stiff brush and soap. Old restorations and glue can easily be removed with solvents. Animal glue or shellac will melt or become softened by soaking in hot water and will separate from the fragments of the vase. Modern plastic cements can be softened with alcohol, benzol, or acetone. Painted restorations will usually yield to one of these solvents or, in stubborn cases, commercial paint remover preparations can be used safely. The plaster additions will crumble after a long soaking in water, or the process can be accelerated by using hydrochloric acid.

The main principle in cleaning a vase covered with earth and encrustations is to recover as much as possible of the ancient surface. The vase or the fragments should be placed in a large basin of water for several weeks, changing the water each day. A water softening agent like Calgon or borax may be used to accelerate the cleaning process. Pure distilled water should be used for the last three days to eliminate dissolved minerals. This prolonged soaking will soften dirt and organic accretions which then can be removed by brushing gently with a soft brush. The soaking will tend to dissolve the salts which may be present in the clay body. If, after drying, a white powdery material again appears on the surface of the vase, it should be brushed off carefully and the vase resoaked for two more weeks. The process may have to be repeated several times.

257

White-ground lekythoi were often decorated with colors which were not fired and are water soluble. These colors must not be soaked. They should be cleaned carefully with small damp cotton swabs, avoiding the drawing on the white-ground as much as possible.

Removing lime

The lime or silica encrustations will not be affected by the soaking and must be removed by other means. They both appear as a white coating and to the eye they are identical. Hydrochloric acid will dissolve a lime encrustation. It may be applied full strength locally with cotton swabs, or the vase may be immersed in a solution of one part hydrochloric acid and twenty parts water. The vase should be thoroughly wet with water before either treatment. The acid will react vigorously with the lime deposit and cause a harmless bubbling around the deposit. The application should be continued until all of the lime is removed. The acid will also remove adhesions of iron rust and bronze deposits. Prolonged washing and soaking will neutralize and remove the acid. Citric or hot oxalic acid is used to bleach and remove the foxing stains caused by decayed vegetable matter. Hydrogen peroxide may also be used at a concentration of 5–25% depending on the intensity of the black stains.

Removing silica

Unfortunately, hydrochloric acid has no effect on a silica encrustation, nor has any other acid that will not harm the black glaze or the clay body as well. Therefore, a silica encrustation has to be removed by mechanical means which involves the painstaking and tedious process of carefully scraping away the encrustation with a very sharp scalpel. The work must be continuously observed through a magnifying glass or irreparable damage can be done to the black glaze. The encrustation and the glaze are of approximately the same hardness; great care must be taken to separate the two.[4]

Refiring

Vases which were placed on funeral pyres were usually broken by the rapid and uneven heating which caused unequal expansion of parts of the vases, resulting in strain and fractures. Those that were broken on a funeral pyre can usually be identified because they tend to have fragments with irregular wavy edges rather than the straight edges caused by normal impact breakage. Often these fragments were badly discolored by carbon smudging from the smoke, and the iron in the clay body was reduced by the lack of oxygen causing a change of color. Such fragments exhibit a grayish body color rather than the customary reddish-orange of Attic pottery (see Chapter Four).

If the temperature of the funeral pyre exceeded 1050°C., the black glaze would reoxidize to red; if the temperature exceeded 1100°C., the clay body of the vase fragments would warp.

Fortunately the majority of vase fragments burned on a funeral pyre are neither warped nor is the black glaze permanently damaged. The fragments which are carbon smudged and reduced are various shades of gray and may even look like a black and white illustration. In some cases vases have been reassembled from these gray fragments, but unfortunately the final result is quite unattractive.

With the exception of the few cases where there has been permanent damage, it is possible to eliminate the disfiguring appearance of these fragments by reversing the chemical process. Basically, this is done by refiring the unattractive gray fragments in an oxidizing atmosphere at a temperature approximating the original firing temperature of the vase; the oxygen in the atmosphere readily enters the porous clay body of the vase and burns away the carbon smudging. In addition the iron oxide in the body of the vase had been reduced to ferrous oxide which contributed to the unattractive gray color. However, in the presence of an abundance of oxygen in the refiring process this black ferrous oxide is reoxidized to red ferric oxide which restores the normal reddish-orange color of Attic pottery. The refired fragments duplicate the original colors and appearance of the vase.[5]

The procedure is as follows. The fragments to be refired are placed on a shelf in the kiln. They may touch each other or overlap provided that all fragments are exposed to the air. The Greek black glaze will not soften or melt at the refiring temperature, therefore, the pieces will not stick to each other. It is important that there is free access to air and consequently oxygen in the kiln. An electric kiln is recommended because it normally fires with an oxidizing atmosphere. Oil-fired or gas-fired kilns may be fired with either an oxidizing or a reducing atmosphere, and therefore, if they are used, care must be taken to make sure that only the oxidizing stage is employed.

The fragments should be heated slowly so that they achieve a temperature of approximately 850°C. after a firing time of about two hours. This slow increase in temperature will make sure that no additional breakage will occur due to strains induced by a rapid rise in temperature. The 850°C. temperature should be maintained about 15 minutes and then the kiln is turned off and allowed to cool slowly. The fragments may be removed about 12 hours later. Using this procedure, there is little danger to the fragments and they will be restored to their original appearance.

Often the fragments of a vase burned on a funeral pyre will be uneven in color. Some pieces may have fallen through the fire and escaped further damage, while others lodged on the blazing pyre will show varying amounts of discoloration. For uniformity it is desirable that all surviving fragments of a vase be refired at the same time.

Certain white-ground vases such as lekythoi were painted after firing with fairly fugitive mineral or vegetable colors. Of course, such a vase will have these colors destroyed if it was burned on a funeral pyre.

If a vase with black glaze had suffered a misfire at the time it was made in antiquity, red or brown spots and streaks may have resulted. They could have been caused by either too low a firing temperature or by a temperature which was too high. I have been able to correct such misfires by using the three-stage firing process exactly as if the pieces had never been fired previously. This involves an oxidizing firing to about 850°C., a reduction firing to about 950°C., cooling under reducing conditions to 875°C. at which point oxygen is permitted to enter the kiln, and the firing concluded so that the kiln cools down under reoxidizing conditions. Both underfired and overfired vases can be corrected and made to have a standard black glaze and to achieve the original appearance that the vase-painter intended.

This does raise the ethical and moral question as to whether it is proper to correct an error made by an ancient potter in firing his kiln several thousand years ago. On the other hand the refiring of vases burnt on a funeral pyre can be justified on the basis that such damage, like breakage, occurred after the vase left the workshop of the potter. From the standpoint of historical accuracy the refiring should be noted in the permanent record of the piece. The vase can no longer be checked for age by the thermoluminescent process as the refiring has erased the radiation strain, and the piece would appear to be modern.

Assembling

The cleaning process having been completed, the next step is to reassemble the pieces. If the vase is in many fragments it becomes a three-dimensional jig-saw puzzle. The scene on the vase is of great help in assembly, as are the foot, mouth, or handles whose specific shapes identify their component parts. The large areas of plain black glaze are the most troublesome. Two clues in identifying the whole are the curves of the fragments and the ridges on the unglazed inside surface which were formed by the potter's fingers as the vase revolved on the wheel. The ridges on a fragment should be aligned parallel to the base of the foot in one of the two possible attitudes (i.e., right side up or upside down) in order to assume the original position. When two fragments seem to fit together, the ridges should be lined up because they must coincide. It is convenient to put a pencil line across two fragments that join for easy reference when they are being glued together.

Cementing

A modern plastic binder may be used, one that can be removed with a solvent.[6] Both edges of the joining fragments should be coated with a thin layer of binder and then allowed to dry slightly until tacky. They should then be pressed firmly together and balanced in a container of dry sand. The weight of one fragment on another maintains the pressure and the sand keeps the fragments from sagging until the cement is strong enough to repeat the process of joining the next piece. Large vases are sometimes assembled around an armature and the pieces are held with rubber bands. Occasionally a long fragment will not fit properly because it has warped or sprung slightly. Such a piece must be sprung and bent a little and clamped in place until the binder dries and holds it firmly. Re-gluing a vase that had been restored previously sometimes reveals that the first restorer scraped the edges of the fragments when he had trouble in making them fit. This creates a difficult task for the modern restorer because the pieces do not fit well and tend to wobble and have gaps between them.

Replacing

Missing fragments are replaced by plaster. To form a piece in the body of a vase, modeling clay is smoothed to a flat surface and then pressed over the hole from the inside of the vase. The plaster, mixed to a stiff consistency, is applied on the outside with a small spatula, and as it dries it is smoothed. The clay readily separates from the plaster and is removed. The following day the plaster should be sandpapered to smooth the final surface. Missing feet and handles are much more difficult to replace. Either they have to be modeled freehand in plaster, turned on a wheel in plaster using a template, or cast in a mold made from a similar vase.

An alternate and superior procedure has been developed at the J. Paul Getty Museum. To fill the void of a missing fragment a rough approximation of the fragment is made from epoxy. The epoxy in a soft doughy state is rolled out to a thickness a little less than the missing fragment. It is then cut to size using a template. After the epoxy has hardened it is trimmed and filed to fit. Then it is cemented in place with Duco cement.

The exterior and interior surfaces are built up with a Polyfilla compound using a small spatula. The Polyfilla compound is marketed as a material to spackle walls. When it hardens it is scraped and sanded to a smooth surface. The epoxy and Polyfilla combination is also used to reproduce missing handles and feet.

Restoring

The attitude toward restoring paintings on vases has changed over the years. In the late nineteenth century vases were restored completely with as much overpaint as was required to present a vase as an intact work of art. The lines between the fragments were filled in and paint was applied freely over the surface of a vase to hide the joints. Missing fragments in the area of a scene on a vase were boldly redrawn, not only completing some figures, often erroneously, but even adding others.

Today a restorer attempts to present the work of an ancient artist in a manner devoid of modern interpretation. Restoration is held to a minimum. Missing fragments are restored in plaster to complete the shape of the vase. They are usually painted either the black of the glaze or the red color of the clay body to harmonize with the balance of the vase. White plaster patches are disconcerting and interfere with an appreciation of the vase-paintings. It is not desirable to draw in missing elements of a vase-painting in a manner imitating the painter's style, or with the intent to complete the drawing, because it confuses the study of the original work and gives a wrong impression. Where it is necessary to complete a geometric form or a line, it is proper to fill in an area as a solid tone, or to continue a broken line, provided that the restoration is immediately apparent. Otherwise the area should be left blank.

Some restorers prefer to tint their plaster with red pigment, before forming a missing piece, to imitate the color of the clay body. This procedure is satisfactory as only the black glaze areas have to be painted later. It does have the disadvantage, however, of weakening the plaster. The plaster surface should be sealed with a coat of shellac before painting, because plaster is very porous. A wide variety of paints can be used; among them are water base paints, conventional artist's oil paints, and oil base enamels. The oil paints unfortunately stain the clay as the oil base seeps into it. A satisfactory paint can be made by grinding mineral colors in damar gum as a medium, using benzol as a solvent. The newest and best technique is the use of acrylic polymer paints which are water soluble and dry to a flexible water-resistant film. Acrylic paints are available in unlimited colors and have a fine adhesive quality. They may be applied directly to Polyfilla restorations. Such restorations should never extend over an ancient painted surface, nor should they be irremovable.

The final step is waxing the vase which closes the surface pores and permits dusting with a moist cloth. This has the further advantage of darkening a dull black glaze and deepening the colors. Any good soft commercial paste wax preparation, composed of a mixture of hard and soft waxes together with a solvent, is satisfactory. After a thin coating has dried it should be polished slightly with a soft cloth. Wax should be used only on black- or red-figured vases, never on white-ground or geometric pottery because the wax will penetrate and discolor them.

Photography

The photography of vases is an area where more standardization is desirable for the purpose of publication in the Corpus Vasorum Antiquorum, etc.[7] Too often a vase is poorly photographed from the wrong viewpoint, not completely in focus, with a distracting background, using an improper lens that distorts the shape, and obscuring the vase drawing by misplaced highlights. All of these elements can be controlled. The background should be a large curved paper sheet of a medium gray tone. The height of the lens of the camera should be half the height of the vase and at right angles to it. The focal length of the lens should be very long so that the camera can be placed at a distance of at least six times the height of the vase. This will produce an excellent silhouette of the vase shape without distortion. The lens should be stopped down to at least f: 32 to insure a sharp image over the entire depth of field. The vase should be photographed in a darkened room illuminated by four or more lights which are covered with Polaroid discs.[8] The lens must also be fitted with a similar disc that polarizes the light, and by rotating and adjusting the discs, all highlights may be canceled. The process works equally well for black and white or color photographs.

A white-ground lekythos or other cylindrical vase with the drawing encircling it presents a difficult photographic problem because only part of the vase drawing can be seen at a time. A very ingenious solution was devised by Arthur Hamilton Smith of the British Museum in 1895: the Cyclograph is a special camera constructed to take a strip photograph of the entire circumference of a vase. The vase is mounted on a revolving stand and while it rotates the film is moved in the opposite direction past a slit behind the stationary lens. The resulting photograph has in effect unrolled the drawing on the vase.

258

259

260

261

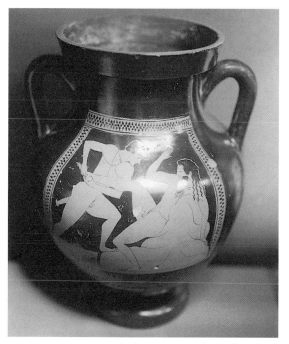

258,259 Two views of the same amphora, by the Gallatin Painter, showing the importance of high-quality photography.

260,261 White-ground lekythos, by the Diosphos Painter; the cyclograph photograph of this vase shows its entire circumference.

THE POEM ENTITLED *KILN*

Translation and notes by Marjorie J. Milne

THIS POEM IS preserved in a *Life of Homer* that purports to be by Herodotus. This *Life* is commonly dated in the second or third century A D, when imitation of the style and dialect of the famous fifth-century historian was fashionable. In the opinion of Wilamowitz, however, its language is quite different from that of such Roman imitations: much of it is Hellenistic Greek, and the Ionic element, he thought, was derived from the sources used by the author, i.e., one or more chapbooks (*Volksbücher*) on the life of Homer, which he had undertaken to modernize. Wilamowitz accordingly dated the pseudo-Herodotean *Life* some time between 130 and 80 B C (see *Die Ilias und Homer* [1916], pp. 413–439).

The work depicts Homer's life as that of a wandering rhapsode. Interspersed in it are a number of short poems in dactylic hexameters, most of which he is represented as having extemporized in the various places that he visited. The one on the kiln is attributed to his stay on Samos. Some potters who were firing a kiln full of fine vases saw him passing by, and, since they had heard that he was a clever man, offered to give him some of the vases and other things besides if he would sing for them. So he sang this song. The author of the pseudo-Herodotean *Life* does not say whether they kept their promise, but passes on to the next episode on Samos. That is, he does not represent the poem as a begging song. Its true character was recognized by Karl Wilhelm Göttling in an article published in 1860. Göttling does not mention the other ancient Greek examples of the genre, but they support his conclusion, especially the Rhodian Swallow Song (Athenaeus VIII, 360 b–d), which is the best preserved.

The Homeric authorship of the poem on the kiln was not universally accepted in antiquity. Some people attributed it to Hesiod, as we are informed by the lexicographer Pollux of the second half of the second century A D (see the critical note on line 3). Both attributions are, of course, worthless. Since Homer was the most famous of early Greek poets and Hesiod was the next most famous and the works of both were composed in dactylic hexameters, there was a strong tendency to attribute anonymous poems in this meter to one or the other of them.

The connection of the poem with Samos probably does not rest on a genuine tradition, for its language has some characteristics that are not Ionic. The author of the *Life* may well have chosen this island as a particularly appropriate place for the origin of such a poem. For from at least as early as 200 BC down into the fourth century AD "Samian vases" are referred to in Roman literature, and the expression often seems to be a literary term for clay, as opposed to metal, vases (see F. O. Waagé, *Antiquity* XI [1937], pp. 46–55, and T. S. Broughton in *An Economic Survey of Ancient Rome* IV [1938], p. 831; in the seventh century AD we even find Isidore of Seville, in his *Etymologiae sive Origines* XX. iv. 3, attributing the invention of clay vases to Samos).

Athens as the place of origin of the poem was suggested by Göttling in the article to which we have already referred, but of his arguments only two are valid, the fact that the first syllables of καλῶς and τέχνη are short (lines 4 and 10), and the great number of potters in the Kerameikos. The results of excavations carried out since his time supply us with another one: Athens remained a center for the making of fine vases for centuries longer than any other spot in the ancient Greek world and would therefore be most likely to *preserve* such a poem. (See further the notes on lines 4, 10, and 23).

The most interesting part of the poem concerns the five maleficent demons, each with his separate function expressed in his name. Syntrips (Smasher), obviously, breaks the pots. Sabaktes (he who scatters or shakes violently) causes a whole stack of them to come tumbling down when the lowest one is broken. Smaragos (Crasher) has been well interpreted by Professor R. M. Cook as the demon who makes pots burst in the kiln, and Asbetos (Unquenchable, Unquenched) as the one who raises too high the heat in the kiln. On Omodamos, Professor Cook has the following comments: "It is less easy to guess the misfortune over which Ὠμόδαμος presides, but some damage to the pot while still unfired – and ὠμός is used in that sense – is more probable than an affliction of the potter's shoulder. I do not think that the general destruction of lines 11–12 is to be assigned to Ὠμόδαμος and, indeed, it is hardly in keeping with the character given him in the preceding line. But anyhow, the beginning of line 11 is corrupt: I should like to restore an optative verb and a noun in the nominative." This, it seems to me, needs both amplification and correction. Certainly the first element of Omodamos' name refers to unfired clay. Now unfired pots while drying outside the kiln are liable to damage, such as, for example, sagging or cracks, and for such damage Omodamos would certainly have been blamed. But the demons are called "ravagers of kilns" and the damage he is here asked to do must therefore take place in the kiln. What can this be? The answer is provided by Aristotle. In *Meteorologica* IV, 380 b, 6ff, while discussing the term ὠμότης he states that substances that are capable of being mastered by heat and thus acquiring consistency but have not been so affected are called ὠμά, and cites potter's clay among the examples. Further on, 383 a, 14ff, he states that compounds of earth and water are hardened (πήγνυται) and made more dense (παχύνεται) both by fire and by cold and that many substances that have been made dense or hard by cold become moist at first (s.c. when heated), such as potter's clay, which, at the beginning of firing, steams and becomes softer. For this reason, he says, it can even become distorted in the kilns. I suggest that the distortion of vases that are in the kiln but are still ὠμά was attributed to Omodamos. What I cannot understand is Professor Cook's statement that "the general destruction of lines 11–12 is hardly in keeping with the character given him in the preceding line;" the preceding line being "and Omodamos, who makes much trouble for this craft." If this destruction would not be regarded by potters as a misfortune, what would? Perhaps what Professor Cook really meant to say was that such a destruction was not in keeping with Omodamos' *name*. The mud and clay of which ancient Greek kilns were largely – sometimes entirely – constructed would have been baked at the first firing and thereafter would have been immune to the attacks of a demon with such a name. To this objection there are three possible answers. (1) This song may have been sung only at the first firing of new kilns. (2) It might, on the other hand, have been sung at the first firing after the end of the rainy season, the kilns being either new or partially repaired. For the potter's craft must in ancient as in modern Greece have been a seasonal one, and the winter rains must then, as now, have damaged some kilns. (3) If ancient potters were in the habit of smearing with fresh clay any cracks that developed in their kilns during the dry season, the song could have been sung at any firing, for the singers could always assume that there might be such freshly smeared cracks for Omodamos to attack. For the modern practice of smearing cracks see Bernard Leach, *A Potter's Book* (1940), p. 216. A vivid description of the repair of a partially ruined modern Greek kiln and its first firing after the repairs is given by R. Hampe and A. Winter in *Bei Töpfern und Töpferinnen in Kreta Messenien und Zypern* (1962), pp. 21–22, 24–25, 35–39. Any one of these three hypotheses would explain why Omodamos is singled out as the demon who makes much trouble for the potter's craft. Though, like each of the others, he has but one function, the nature of his function allows him to ruin not only pots but kilns as well. The kiln that is to be destroyed is described in the phrase "*pyraithousa* and chambers." The word *pyraithousa* occurs nowhere else: it is a compound formed from the noun *pyr* meaning "fire" and the feminine active participle of the verb *aithein* meaning "to kindle," or sometimes "to blaze." There is no other example in Greek of a compound of this type meaning place where such-and-such a thing is done; we should expect the word for "place where the fire is kindled or blazes" to be *pyraitheion*, and that word is, in fact, used of the Persian fire-temples. I suggest, therefore, that the literal meaning of *pyraithousa* is "fire-porch," for *aithousa* is the Homeric word for porch and in the representations of kilns on the votive tablets from Penteskouphia the stoking tunnel, open in front, closed on top and sides, has the form of a rude porch. The "chambers" are the upper and lower chambers of the kiln itself. The verb that precedes *pyraithousa* is corrupt in the manuscripts: my reasons for preferring Wilamowitz's emendation *steibe*, "stamp on," are given in the note on line 11. 232

From these demons it is indeed a far cry to such mythological characters as Circe and the Centaurs, and Wilamowitz was undoubtedly right in seeing here the hand of a later poet. He may have belonged to the Hellenistic period, when allusions to little-known local myths were a literary fashion. For he speaks of the Centaurs who escaped the hands of Herakles, and in the standard mythology none of them did. But Apollodorus, *Bibliotheca* II.5.4, tells us that some fled to a certain mountain (the name of which is corrupt) and that others were received at Eleusis by Poseidon, who covered them with a mountain. The passage is discussed by Wilamowitz (not, however, in connection with this poem) in *Der Glaube der Hellenen* I (1931), p. 396, note 1, who remarks that, if the name Eleusis is genuine, it must refer to a Laconian Eleusis, not the Attic one. That the story of the escape of these Centaurs was a Laconian myth is made probable by Apollodorus' statement that at the time of the pursuit Cheiron was living in Malea (for the geography see Wilamowitz, op. cit. pp. 396–7). The only trace we have, moreover, of a cult of Cheiron is an inscription on Thera (*I. G.* XII, fasc. 3, no. 360), an island the Lacedaemonians claimed, at least, to have colonized.

Note on begging songs. The Rhodian Swallow Song is preserved in Athenaeus, *Deipnosophistae* VIII, 360 c–d; for English translations see C. B. Gulick's edition of Athenaeus in the Loeb Classical Library, vol. IV, p. 131, and J. M. Edmonds, *Lyra Graeca* in the same series, vol. III, pp. 527 and 529. A badly preserved *Eiresione* ("sung to tatters" [*zersungen*] is Wilamowitz's vivid description) is included in the pseudo-Herodotean *Life of Homer* and is there said to be Samian: for English translations see H. G. Evelyn-White, *Hesiod, the Homeric Hymns, and Homerica* in the Loeb series, p. 475, and J. M. Edmonds, op. cit., pp. 523 and 525. Two passages from a Crow Song by the Hellenistic poet Phoenix of Colophon are quoted by Athenaeus VIII, 359 e–360 a, and are translated by Gulick, op. cit. IV, pp. 127 and 129.

The poem

The text here reproduced is that of Wilamowitz in his *Vitae Homeri et Hesiodi* (Bonn, 1916), pp. 17–18. At the beginning of line 11, however, I have substituted for πεῖθε, which he prints, marking it with a dagger, the sign of textual corruption, his own conjecture στεῖβε, which I am convinced is right (see below, in the section, "Notes on the Text and the Translation").

Εἰ μὲν δώσετε μισθὸν ἀοιδῆς, ὦ κεραμῆες,
δεῦρ' ἄγ' Ἀθηναίη καὶ ὑπέρσχεθε χεῖρα καμίνου,
εὖ δὲ μελανθεῖεν κότυλοι καὶ πάντα κάναστρα,
φρυχθῆναί τε καλῶς καὶ τιμῆς ὦνον ἀρέσθαι,
5   πολλὰ μὲν εἰν ἀγορῆι πωλεύμενα πολλὰ δ' ἀγυιαῖς,
πολλὰ δὲ κερδῆναι, ἡμῖν δ' ἡδέως σφιν ἀεῖσαι.
ἢν δ' ἐπ' ἀναιδείην τρεφθέντες ψεύδε' ἄρησθε,
συγκαλέω δὴ ἔπειτα καμίνων δηλητῆρας
Σύντριβ' ὁμῶς Σμάραγόν τε καὶ Ἄσβετον ἠδὲ Σαβάκτην
10 Ὠμόδαμόν θ', ὃς τῆιδε τέχνηι κακὰ πολλὰ πορίζει·
στεῖβε πυραίθουσαν καὶ δώματα· σὺν δὲ κάμινος
πᾶσα κυκηθείη, κεραμέων μέγα κωκυσάντων.
ὡς γνάθος ἱππείη βρύκει βρύκοι δὲ κάμινος
πάντ' ἔντοσθ' αὐτῆς κεραμήϊα λεπτὰ ποοῦσα.
15 δεῦρο καὶ Ἡελίου θύγατερ, πολυφάρμακε Κίρκη,
ἄγρια φάρμακα βάλλε, κάκου δ' αὐτούς τε καὶ ἔργα·
δεῦρο δὲ καὶ Χείρων ἀγέτω πολέας Κενταύρους,
οἵ θ' Ἡρακλῆος χεῖρας φύγον οἵ τ' ἀπόλοντο·
τύπτοιεν τάδε ἔργα κακῶς, πίπτοι δὲ κάμινος.
20 αὐτοὶ δ' οἰμώζοντες ὁρώιατο ἔργα πονηρά.
γηθήσω δ' ὁρόων αὐτῶν κακοδαίμονα τέχνην.
ὃς δέ χ' ὑπερκύψηι, περὶ τούτου πᾶν τὸ πρόσωπον
φλεχθείη, ὡς πάντες ἐπίστωντ' αἴσιμα ῥέζειν.

If you will pay me for my song, O potters,
then come, Athena, and hold thy hand above the kiln!
May the kotyloi and all the kanastra turn a good black,
may they be well fired and fetch the price asked,
5   many being sold in the marketplace and many on the roads,
and bring in much money, and may my song be pleasing.
But if you (potters) turn shameless and deceitful,
then do I summon the ravagers of kilns,
both Syntrips (Smasher) and Smaragos (Crasher) and
        Asbetos (Unquenchable) too, and Sabaktes (Shake-to-Pieces)

10 and Omodamos (Conqueror of the Unbaked), who makes
      much trouble for this craft.
  Stamp on stoking tunnel and chambers, and may the whole kiln
  be thrown into confusion, while the potters loudly wail.
  As grinds a horse's jaw so may the kiln grind
  to powder all the pots within it.
15 [Come, too, daughter of the Sun, Circe of many spells,
  cast cruel spells, do evil to them and their handiwork.
  Here too let Cheiron lead many Centaurs,
  both those that escaped the hands of Herakles and those that perished.
  May they hit these pots hard, and may the kiln collapse.
20 And may the potters wail as they see the mischief.
  But I shall rejoice at the sight of their luckless craft.]
  And if anyone bends over to look into the spy-hole, may his whole face
  be scorched, so that all may learn to deal justly.

Notes on the text and the translation

The pseudo-Herodotean *Life of Homer* is included in the first edition of Homer, edited by Demetrius Chalcondyles of Athens and printed at Florence in 1488. The principal modern editions of this *Life* are those of Westermann in his Βιογράφοι, *Vitarum Scriptores Graeci Minores* (1845), T. W. Allen in the fifth volume of his Oxford text of Homer (1912), and Ulrich von Wilamowitz-Moellendorff in his *Vitae Homeri et Hesiodi in Usum Scholarum* (Bonn, 1916). The poem on the kiln is also found in the short life of Homer in the lexicon of Suidas; for this see Ada Adler's edition of Suidas, s. v. Ὅμηρος.

Besides the above works I have consulted Karl Wilhelm Göttling's Jena University program of 1860 (reprinted in his *Opuscula Academica* [1869], pp. 182–188), which was in some respects far ahead of its time, the pertinent part of Arthur Ludwich's article "Homerische Gelegenheitsdichtungen" in *Rheinisches Museum für Philologie*, n. s. LXXI (1916), which is valuable for its account of the manuscript readings, and R. M. Cook's articles in *The Classical Review* LXII (1948), pp. 55–57, and n. s. I (1951), p. 9.

In the following notes the variant readings and emendations mentioned concern only ancient pottery, the names and activities of the demons, and the date of the poem. For the others readers are referred to the editions of Westermann and Wilamowitz (that of Allen is more a hindrance than a help), pp. 206–213 of Ludwich's article in *Rheinisches Museum* LXXI (1916), Ada Adler's edition of Suidas, and Professor Cook's article in *The Classical Review* LXII (1948).

Line 3. μελανθεῖεν (may they turn black), pseudo-Herodotus; μαρανθεῖεν Suidas; περανθεῖεν Pollux X. 85, who quotes this line. Gottfried Hermann in his edition of the Homeric Hymns and Epigrams, published in Leipzig in 1806, ("epigrams" being the conventional name for the short poems in the pseudo-Herodotean *Life*) preferred περανθεῖεν and has been followed by most editors of these poems. Göttling, however, in 1860 had the sagacity to prefer μελανθεῖεν, citing the black glaze as an argument. When in 1916 Wilamowitz did the same, Ludwich attacked him bitterly in his review (*Berliner philologische Wochenschrift* XXXVII [1917], col. 533), arguing that vases were not put in the kiln in order to turn a good black but to be made hard, so that they would be usable and salable. It was not until 1942, when Dr Theodor Schumann succeeded in reproducing the Greek black glaze, that μελανθεῖεν was proved right. The explanation of the reading περανθεῖεν in Pollux is obvious. In the second or possibly the late third century BC red ware (the so-called Pergamene or Sigillata) was introduced and in the first two centuries AD became universally popular. Hence the prayer, "May they turn a good black," was changed to the rather pallid "May they turn out well." κάναστρα Pollux X. 85; μάλ' ἱρά pseudo-Herodotus and Suidas (some manuscripts of pseudo-Herodotus and one of Suidas have ἱερά instead of ἱρά). Kanastron is defined by the lexicographer Hesychius as "a terracotta vase, a bowl, a basket." It is used of terracotta vases in an inscription from Lebena, Crete, of the second century BC (Collitz and others, *Sammlung der griechischen Dialektinschriften*, 5087 a, line 9, republished by M. Guarducci, *Inscriptiones Creticae* I, xvii, 2; the translation "wicker basket" in Liddell and Scott is a mistake.) It also appears in a variant spelling on an inscribed sherd found at Naucratis and now in the Fitzwilliam Museum, Cambridge (no. N 99–N 104 *a*), which was published by C. C. Edgar (who noted its relevance to the quotation in Pollux) in *BSA* V (1898–9), p. 56, no. III, pl. V, and republished in 1923 by Schwyzer in *Dialectorum Graecarum exempla epigraphica potiora*, no. 748, 3, who called it Ionic, obviously because of its finding place. In 1951 both sherd and inscription were identified as Attic. Mr Peter Corbett dated the sherd, which is the base of a "one-handler" (see ills 262, 263 for an example of this shape), in the first quarter of the fourth century BC or "slightly less probably" in the last quarter of the fifth. Mr G. Woodhead said the forms and values of the letters suggest a date in the second half of the fifth century. The *graffito* reads Αρτομονος το κανασθον τοτο "This is the kanasthon of Artomon." The writer was a bad speller, as Edgar noted. His name was probably Artemon, and kanasthon should certainly have been spelled kanasthron (for this type of spelling mistake see Meisterhans and Schwyzer, *Grammatik der attischen Inschriften*, pp. 81 f., 4 b, and note 703). The suffixes -τρον and -θρον have the same meaning and in some words are interchangeable; see Schwyzer, *Griechische Grammatik* I (1939), p. 532, 3,

262, 263

262,263 Profile and exterior view of a kanastron from the Athenian Agora, 475–450 BC.

where the various spellings of κάναστρον are recorded, and p. 533, 36. Professor Cook, who published the results of Mr Corbett's and Mr Woodhead's examination of the sherd in *The Classical Review* n. s. 1 (1951), p. 9, concludes, with what seems to me excessive caution, "The ancient name for these one-handled cups, which are normally painted black, is not determined, and 'κάνασθον', like κότυλος, may have a general rather than a particular significance." "Basket" would seem to be the original meaning of the word (cf. kaneon, "basket" and kanathron or kannathron, "a cane or wicker carriage"). Probably it was used of baskets of some particular shape and was then given to terracotta vases (and those of other materials) that more or less resembled that shape. These vases were apparently not cups, for Pollux mentions them along with various dishes in which food was served. The description "wide open" (or "spread out") "like phialae" (ταῦτα δὲ ὅσα κατὰ φιάλας ἀνεπέπτατο) which he gives in vi. 86 of the kanastra mentioned by the Athenian comic poet Nikophon, who was active from *c*.410 to 388 BC or later, exactly fits the shallow bowls of the one-handlers. I therefore see no reason to doubt that the *graffito* on the Cambridge sherd gives us the Attic name of this Attic shape. I say "the Attic name" rather than "the ancient name," for some vase names were applied to certain shapes in certain localities and to entirely different shapes in others (and the same may have been true of basket names, about which we have much less information). Now Pollux's Atticism was of the type that included famous non-Attic writers among its models. The question therefore arises whether the unnamed ultimate source for the definition "cork pinakiskoi" that he gives of *kanastra* in x. 85 was Attic. It is not impossible, however, that these pinakiskoi were one-handlers, for they may have been not flat plates but shallow bowls (cf. the κοῖλοι πίνακες he mentions in x. 82). It would seem, indeed, that Pollux himself took them to be bowls, for he adds, "whence they say *kanaxai* and *ekkanaxai* for 'empty' or 'drink up' " (the etymology, like so many ancient ones, is false). It must be remembered, however, that our text of Pollux is merely an epitome of the lost original, and the etymology may have been attached to something omitted by the epitomizer. For information on the date of the one-handlers I have to thank Miss Lucy Talcott, who writes in a letter of 25 February 1965: "This useful and very popular shape first appears about 520 BC and continues until near the end of the fourth century," and adds, "The last catalogued example of the ordinary variety is of *c.* 325 BC, though some variant shapes may be as late as *c.* 325–310." (See ills 262, 263: a kanastron from the Athenian Agora, no. P15998, 475–450 BC.) If, therefore, this poem was composed in Athens, any time between *c.* 520 and *c.* 325 BC would be a possible date. In view, however, of its general character, I think it is more likely to belong to the archaic period and therefore suggest *c.* 520–*c.* 480 BC. When the popularity of the one-handler ceased, or perhaps even before its end, another vase name was substituted by the singers, which, through being sung by successive generations, became the nonsensical μάλ᾽ ἱρά, "very sacred things." How then was the original vase name preserved? The poem may have been included in a book while κάναστρα still remained in the text, for in the fifth and fourth centuries BC Athens was the center of the book trade. περανθεῖεν, on this hypothesis, would have been a "correction" made probably in the Roman age by someone to whom μελανθεῖεν didn't make sense.

Line 4. The α of καλῶς is short as in Attic. In East and Central Ionic it was long, but it is sometimes short in post-Homeric Ionian poetry (Schwyzer, *Griechische Grammatik* I [1934], p. 228, 3).

Line 9. Ἄσβετον is Stephanos' emendation. The manuscripts have ἄσβεστον. σαβάκτην Parisinus 2626, the oldest Suidas manuscript (twelfth century); γ᾽ ἄβακτον Vaticanus gr. 305 (beginning of the fourteenth century); γ᾽ ἄμακτον Parisinus 2766 (fourteenth century), the older part (fourteenth century) of Lipsiensis (1275) 32, and Palatino-Vatican. 310 (fifteenth century). That is, the name of the fourth demon was Sabaktes, and Amaktos

262, 263

is merely a guess made by someone who thought (quite rightly) that the corrupt Abaktos (meaning "not to be deemed happy") was not a suitable name for a demon of this kind.

Line 10. The first syllable of τέχνη is scanned as short here. Such treatment of a short vowel followed by a mute and a liquid or a mute and a nasal is common in Attic poetry, but Ionian poets tend to avoid such shortenings, especially when the mute is followed by a nasal.

Line 11. στεῖλαι Parisinus 2626 (the twelfth-century Suidas manuscript); πεῖθε Parisinus 2766 (fourteenth century), Vatican. gr. 305 (beginning of the fourteenth century), Palatino-Vatican. 310 (fifteenth century). Evidently the medieval copyists took πυραίθουσαν to be the name of a female fire-demon (as did Ludwich later). They therefore substituted for the imperative with which the line began, and which must have meant "damage" (in some way) or "destroy" (a structure), conjectures of their own, the unmetrical στεῖλαι (send for) of the Suidas manuscripts and πεῖθε (persuade) in the manuscripts of pseudo-Herodotus. For the latter Scaliger conjectured πέρθε (sack) and Portus πρῆθε (blow into a flame); πέρθε has found favor with modern editors. But this (like πρῆθε) is merely an emendation of an emendation. The original word, besides ending in ε, probably had ει in the first syllable, like στεῖλαι and πεῖθε. Wilamowitz's conjecture στεῖβε (stamp on) not only meets this requirement; it also, as he remarked, suits the activity of Omodamos. For this "subduer of unfired clay" would have been imagined by ancient Greek potters as attacking it with his feet, since they themselves kneaded clay with their feet (see Herodotus II. 36; the passage is mistranslated in A. D. Godley's Loeb edition).

Lines 13–14. βρύκειν, "to eat greedily," is translated in this passage "champ the bit" in the last edition of Liddell and Scott. This is not possible, for a horse that champs the metal bit does not destroy it, and the singers are praying for the total destruction of the pots. For λεπτά cf. the Greek original of the proverb "The mills of the gods grind slowly but they grind exceeding small," Ὀψὲ θεῶν ἀλέουσι μύλοι, ἀλέουσι δὲ λεπτά (Leutsch and Schneidewin, *Corpus paroemiographorum Graecorum* I, p. 444, no. 48; II, p. 199 no. 85). Evelyn-White apparently had this proverb in mind when, in his Loeb edition of Hesiod, the Homeric Hymns, and Homerica, he translated "grind to powder." I have adopted his translation, for it gives the spirit of the original better than a literal one could. Powder, Mr Noble informs me, is all that is left of a vase that explodes in the kiln. λέπτ' ἀπολοῦσα "destroying the fine pots," proposed by Professor Cook, would take the life out of the passage. ποοῦσα is the reading of Vatican. gr. 305, and Palatino-Vatican. 310, and is a correction in the twelfth-century Suidas manuscript Parisinus 2626.

Lines 22–23. I quote from Mr Noble the explanation of what happens to the man at the spy-hole: "When a kiln is being fired under reducing conditions, with a lack of oxygen in the kiln, and the spy-hole is suddenly opened, there is often a delayed burst of blue flame from the spy-hole. If the potter is unwary and has his eye too close to the hole he will be burned seriously."

Line 23. ἐπίστωντ' the older part of Codex Lipsiensis (1275) 32, Parisinus 2766, Palatino-Vatican. 310; ἐπίσταντ' Vatican. gr. 305; ἐπίστωνται Parisinus 2626 (the twelfth-century Suidas manuscript). The reading ἐπίσταιντ' is found only in inferior manuscripts but was adopted by most editors before 1916. (The exceptions I have noted are Göttling in his 1860 Jena University program, Eugen Abel in his edition of the Homeric Hymns and Epigrams and the Batrachomyomachia [Leipzig and Prague, 1886], and H. G. Evelyn-White in his *Hesiod, the Homeric Hymns and Homerica* [London and New York, 1914] in the Loeb Classical Library.) It was this reading that caused Wackernagel to say that the poem must have originated either in Attica itself or in a place where Attic speech was current. The parallels he cited for this form of the optative (in -αιντο instead of the Ionic and early Attic -αιατο) would date the poem no earlier than the time of Euripides and Aristophanes. When he wrote this he had no way of knowing that the reading did not have good manuscript support. His article was published in *Glotta* VII (1916) and republished, the same year, as the first 159 pages of his book *Sprachliche Untersuchungen zu Homer* (the page references for his remarks on -αιντο are 252–254 in *Glotta* and 92–94 in *Sprachliche Untersuchungen*). In the same year Ludwich's article, the first really thorough and accurate account of the best manuscripts of the poems in the pseudo-Herodotean *Life of Homer*, was published in the *Rheinisches Museum* in two sections. The poem on the kiln is in the second section. A note dated "June 1916," appended to the preface of Wilamowitz's *Vitae Homeri et Hesiodi* indicates that at that time the second section of Ludwich's article had not yet come out. Now Wackernagel in the preface to his *Spachliche Untersuchungen* says that Wilamowitz's *Ilias und Homer* (also published in 1916, but before *Vitae Homeri et Hesiodi*, to which it refers, on p. 413, as being ready for the press) had come to his attention only when he was correcting his last proofs. Hence it is clear that he could not have seen either Wilamowitz's text of the poem (which adopts the reading ἐπίστωντ') or Ludwich's account of the manuscripts. Wilhelm Schmid in his *Geschichte der griechischen Literatur* I (1929) refers both to Wilamowitz's edition of the *Vitae* (on p. 84, note 7) and to Ludwich's article (on p. 224, note 1) but apparently did not consult either of them on this poem, for he mentions Wackernagel's dating of it without comment (p. 226, note 1).

Tables

Graphs

Notes to the Text

Sources of Illustrations

Index

Table I

Spectrographic analyses of six clays

	Column 1	Column 2	Column 3	Column 4	Column 5	Column 6
	5TH-CENTURY BC ATTIC CLAY	MODERN CLAY FROM ATHENS	MODERN CLAY FROM CHALKIS	MODERN CLAY FROM AEGINA	4TH-CENTURY BC SOUTH ITALIAN CLAY	5TH-CENTURY BC ETRUSCAN CLAY
Silicon	Major	Major	Major	Major	Major	Major
Aluminum	Major (low)	Major	Major	Major	Major	Minor
Iron	Major (low)	Minor (high)	Minor (high)	Minor (high)	Minor	Minor
Titanium	O.X (high)	Minor (low)	Minor (low)	Minor (low)	O.X (low)	O.X
Magnesium	Minor	O.X	O.X	Minor	Major	O.X.
Calcium	Minor	Minor	Minor (low)	Major (low)	Major	O.X (low)
Copper	O.OOX	O.OOX	O.OOX	O.OOX	O.OOX	O.OOX
Potassium	O.X (low)	Minor (low)	Minor (low)	Minor (low)	Not tested	Not found
Manganese	O.X	O.X (low)	O.X (low)	O.X (low)	O.OOX	O.X
Sodium	O.OX	O.OX (low)	O.X (low)	O.OX	O.X	Not found
Lead	O.OOX	O.OOX	O.OOX	O.OOX	O.OOX	O.OOX
Zinc	O.OX	Not found	Not found	Not found	Not found	Not found
Tin	Not found	Not found	Not found	Not found	Not found	Not found
Nickel	O.OOX	O.OOX	O.OOX (low)	O.OX (low)	Not found	Not found
Chromium	O.OOX	O.OX (low)	O.OOX	O.OX (low)	Not found	Not found
Barium	O.OOX	O.X (low)	O.OX	O.OX (low)	Not tested	Not found
Vanadium	Not found	O.OOX	O.OOX	O.OOX	Not found	Not found
Silver	Not found	Not found	Not found	Not found	Not found	Not found
Zirconium	Not tested	O.OOX	O.OOX	O.OOX	Not found	Not tested

Elements checked but not found: Antimony, Arsenic, Bismuth, Cadmium, Cobalt, Indium, Lithium, Molybdenum, Tungsten.
Note:

Major = above 5% estimated.
Minor = 1-5% estimated.
.X, .OX, .OOX, etc. = concentration of the elements estimated to the nearest decimal place, e.g. .OX = .01 - .09% estimated.
The numbers in parentheses indicate the estimated relative concentration of the elements among the various samples.
The elements are listed in the order of their frequency in the samples.
The elements not found are listed in alphabetical order.

TABLE II

*Comparison of spectrographic analyses of
5th-century BC clay and black glaze*

	5TH-CENTURY BC ATTIC CLAY	5TH-CENTURY BC ATTIC BLACK GLAZE
Silicon	Major	Major
Aluminum	Major (low)	Major
Iron	Major (low)	Major
Titanium	O.X (high) (1)	Minor (2)
Magnesium	Minor (1)	Minor (2)
Calcium	Minor (1)	Minor (1)
Copper	O.OOX	O.X (high)
Potassium	O.X (low)	O.X (high)
Manganese	O.X	O.X
Sodium	O.OX	O.X
Lead	O.OOX	O.X (low)
Zinc	O.OX	O.X (low)
Tin	Not found	O.OX
Nickel	O.OOX	O.OX
Chromium	O.OOX	O.OX
Barium	O.OOX	O.OX
Vanadium	Not found	O.OX (low)
Silver	Not found	O.OOX

Elements checked but not found: Antimony, Arsenic,
Bismuth, Cadmium, Cobalt, Indium, Lithium,
Molybdenum, Strontium, Tungsten.

TABLE III

*Spectrographic analyses of modern Attic clay
and modern black glaze made from it*

	MODERN CLAY FROM ATHENS	MODERN BLACK GLAZE
Silicon	Major	Major
Aluminum	Major	Major
Iron	Minor (high)	Major
Titanium	Minor (low)	O.X
Magnesium	O.X	Minor
Calcium	Minor	Major (low)
Copper	O.OOX	O.OX
Potassium	Minor (low)	Major (low)
Manganese	O.X (low)	O.X
Sodium	O.OX (low)	Minor
Lead	O.OOX	O.X
Zinc	Not found	Not found
Tin	Not found	Not found
Nickel	O.OOX	O.X (low)
Chromium	O.OX (low)	O.X (low)
Barium	O.X (low)	O.X (high)
Vanadium	O.OOX	O.OX
Silver	Not found	O.OOX (low)
Zirconium	O.OOX	Not found
Strontium	O.OOX	O.OX
Cobalt	Not found	O.OX (low)

Elements checked but not found: Antimony, Arsenic,
Bismuth, Cadmium, Indium, Lithium, Molybdenum,
Tungsten.

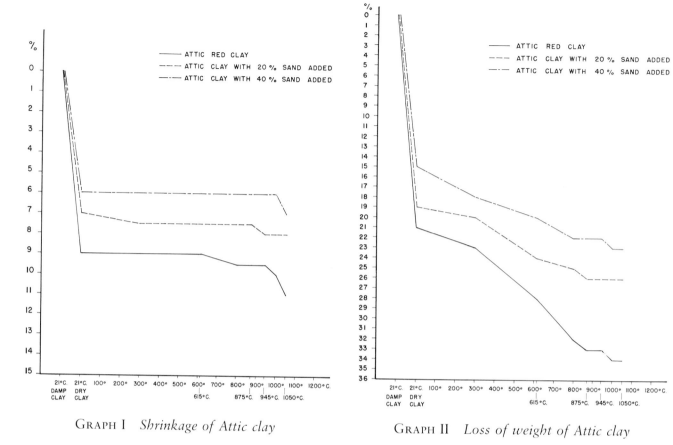

GRAPH I   *Shrinkage of Attic clay*

GRAPH II   *Loss of weight of Attic clay*

GRAPH III   *Hardness of fired Attic clay*

Notes to the Text

PREFACE

1 The following books and articles are some of the most useful studies in the field:

I J. D. Beazley, "Potter and Painter in Ancient Athens," *Proceedings of the British Academy* 30 (1946) 87–125.

II Charles F. Binns and A. D. Fraser, "The Genesis of the Greek Black Glaze," *American Journal of Archaeology* 33 (1929) 1–9, pls I and II. Contains excellent early bibliography.

III Hansjörg Bloesch, "Stout and Slender in the Late Archaic Period," *Journal of Hellenic Studies* 71 (1951) 29–39.

IV Marie Farnsworth and Harriet Wisely, "Fifth Century Intentional Red Glaze," *American Journal of Archaeology* 62 (1958) 165–73, pl. 36 and color plate.

V Marie Farnsworth, "Types of Greek Glaze Failure," *Archaeology* 12 (1959) 242–50.

VI Marie Farnsworth, "Draw Pieces as Aids to Correct Firing," *American Journal of Archaeology* 64 (1960) 72–75, pl. 16.

VII F. Oberlies and N. Köppen, "Untersuchungen an Terra Sigillata und griechischen Vasen," *Berichte der deutschen keramischen Gesellschaft* 30 (1953) 102–110. Also by the same authors in the same publication: "Tonüberzüge, ein Veredlungsverfahren für Keramiken" 31 (1954) 287–301; "Untersuchungen an griechischen Gefässfragmenten aus verschiedenen Jahrhunderten v. Chr." 39 (1962) 19–31.

VIII Gisela M. A. Richter, *The Craft of Athenian Pottery* (1923). Contains many representations of ancient potters and painters, and references to the pottery craft in ancient literature.

Sir John Beazley reviewed this book in *The Burlington Magazine* XLVI (1925) 254, and stated: "Thanks to her double training, as an archeologist and as a potter, she is able to speak with real authority, and she gives a clearer and better account of the process by which an Attic vase must have been produced than can be found anywhere else." He concluded his review with the following, "It is the sort of book that subsequent writers will pillage freely, sometimes with acknowledgments." Time has borne out the truth in both of these statements.

IX Gisela M. A. Richter, *Attic Red-Figured Vases: a Survey* (1946); revised edition (1958).

X T. Schumann, "Oberflächenverzierung in der antiken Töpferkunst. Terra sigillata und griechische Schwarzrotmalerei" *Berichte der deutschen keramischen Gesellschaft* 23 (1942) 408–26. Summarized by Carl Weickert "Zur Technik der griechischen Vasenmalerei" *Arch. Anzeiger* (1942) cols 512–28. These articles did not become available outside continental Europe until after 1945.

XI Adam Winter, "Terra Sigillata und andere antike Glanztontechniken" *Keramische Zeitschrift*, vol. 8, no. 3 (1956) 110–13, and five additional articles in the same journal; vol. 8, no. 8 (1956) 392–93; vol. 8, no. 10 (1956) 513–17; vol. 8, no. 12 (1956) 614–15; vol. 9, no. 1 (1957) 14–16; vol. 9, no. 5 (1957) 258–59. Schumann's untimely death left a void which in Germany was filled by Adam Winter who in many ways went beyond Schumann's initial studies.

XII Adam Winter, "Die Technik des griechischen Töpfers in ihren Grundlagen" *Technische Beiträge zur Archäologie*, Mainz (1959). Contains excellent diagrams of ancient kilns.

2 The reproduction of the Attic relief line was described in a paper read by the author at the Sixty-first General Meeting of the Archaeological Institute of America, 29 December 1959, in New York. This paper was later published with additions in the *American Journal of Archaeology*, 64:4 (October 1960) 307–318, pls 84–87, plus color plate.

3 H. A. G. Brijder (ed.), *Ancient Greek and Related Pottery: Proceedings of the International Vase Symposium Amsterdam 1984*, Allard Pierson Series vol. 5 (1984).

4 Margaret Ellen Mayo (ed.), *The Art of South Italy: Vases from Magna Graecia*, Virginia Museum (1982).

5 Dietrich von Bothmer, *The Amasis Painter and His World: Vase-Painting in Sixth-Century BC Athens*, The J. Paul Getty Museum (1985).

6 Suzanne P. Murray, *Collecting the Classical Past: Antiquities from the Joseph Veach Noble Collection*, Tampa Museum of Art (1985, second edition 1986).

INTRODUCTION

1 Translation by Brian F. Cook.

2 J. D. Beazley, "Potter and Painter in Ancient Athens," *Proceedings of the British Academy* 30 (1946) 87–125.

3 Roland Hampe, *Ein Frühattischer Grabfund* (1960) 45.

4 Attic loutrophoros in The University Museum, Philadelphia, acc. no. 30.4.1; *Museum Journal*, 23, 4–22; J. D. Beazley, *Attic Red-figure Vase-painters* second edition (1963) 990, no. 45.

5 The potter-painter Phintias spelled his name four different ways on his vases; Phintias, Philtias, Phintis and Phitias.

A modern example from an indigenous culture

clearly illustrates some of the problems involved in signatures and why a potter may work with a series of vase-painters. The American Indian potter, Maria Montoya Martinez, was born about 1881 in the San Ildefonso Pueblo in New Mexico. In 1908, she began making pottery which was decorated by her husband, Julian, a collaboration which continued for thirty-five years until his death in 1943. For the next three years, Maria worked with her daughter-in-law, Santana, who painted the vases. When her son, Popovi-Da, returned from the Army in 1946 at the close of World War II he assumed the role of the painter.

Maria began to sign her pottery in 1923 as "Marie," then in 1925 as "Marie and Julian;" however, some pottery was unsigned as late as 1926. It is interesting to note that the name of the potter was signed first and then the painter, which is the logical order. The double signature of "Marie and Santana" was used when they worked together, and lastly, "Maria and Popovi." Maria signed her name "Marie" for many years because she felt it was better known than "Maria" to English-speaking customers. Adding to the confusion is the fact that for some time Maria permitted other potters in her pueblo to sign her name to their pots in order to help them sell their work more readily.

6   Gisela M. A. Richter, *Attic Red-Figured Vases: a Survey* (1946); revised edition (1958) 16–18, and J.D. Beazley, "Potter and Painter in Ancient Athens," *Proceedings of the British Academy* 30 (1946) 87–125. J. D. Beazley, *Attic Red-figure Vase-painters* (1942) second edition (1963), *Attic Black-figure Vase-painters* (1956), and *Paralipomena* (1971).

7   Hansjörg Bloesch, *Formen attischer Schalen von Exekias bis zum Ende des strengen Stils* (1940), and by the same author "Stout and Slender in the Late Archaic Period," *Journal of Hellenic Studies* 71 (1951) 29–39; and "Ein Meisterwerk Der Töpferei," *Antike Kunst* 5 Jahrgang (1962) Heft 1, 18–29.

8   J. D. Beazley, *Attic Black-figure Vase-painters* (1956) 362, no. 36.

9   J. D. Beazley, *Attic Red-figure Vase-painters* second edition (1963) 571, no. 73.

10 D. A. Amyx, *Hesperia* XXVII, 3 (1958) and XXVII, 4 (1958), "The Attic Stelai, Part III."

11 *Journal of Hellenic Studies* LI (1931) 123, J. D. Beazley review of *Corpus Vasorum Antiquorum; British Museum, fasc. 6*: Concerning a *graffito* on the foot of the red-figured hydria shown in pl. 83, "The author translates 'a hydria for 5 drachmae 1 obol,' and refers to Hackl, pp. 51 and 71."

12 Aristophanes, *Frogs*, 1236.

13 Amphora by Euthymides, in the Museum antiker Kleinkunst, Munich 2307 (J. 378).

14 R. M. Cook, *Greek Painted Pottery* (1960), 274–5. T. B. L. Webster, *Potter and Patron In Classical Athens* (1972).

CHAPTER ONE: FORMING THE VASES

1   Daniel Rhodes, *Clay and Glazes for the Potter* (1957), presents a comprehensive description of ceramic chemistry.

2   It is interesting to speculate on what the history of Athens would have been if it were not for the coincidence and chance availability of two famous natural resources, pentelic marble, and good red clay. The choice of the city site in prehistoric times was predicated on the high rocky acropolis, a place of refuge relatively easy to defend, rather than on the convenience of construction and ceramic supplies. How difficult it is to imagine Athens without either marble buildings or beautiful pottery!

3   Humfry Payne, *Necrocorinthia* (1931), 116. *Antike Denkmaeler* I, pl. 8, no. 7.

4   All of the spectrographic analyses were made by Lucius Pitkin, Inc., New York, N. Y. Emission spectrometry requires the destruction of a small sample, about 10 milligrams, of the material being analyzed. Either an expendable sherd is used, or a sample of the clay body is taken by scraping the inside of a vase or under the foot. The black glaze is removed from an inconspicuous spot. The results are the most accurate obtainable because the entire sample is analyzed and not just the surface which may not be typical. x-ray fluorescent spectrometry is an entirely nondestructive analyzing system for pottery which does not harm the piece under study and will yield fairly good results rapidly. However, the readings, made only of the surfaces, are not so accurate as the emission spectrometry system which has been used exclusively for the material in this book.

5   An excellent study of pottery production is given in Anna O. Shepard, *Ceramics for the Archaeologist* (1956). Although the main emphasis of the book is on American pre-Columbian pottery which was made without the use of the potter's wheel, much of the content is applicable to Greek pottery.

The effects of the aging of clay have often been discussed, and it may be that the minute plates in the clay become magnetically oriented in parallel planes which helps its cohesive qualities. Bacterial action seems to help the malleability. Chinese potters prefer long aging of the clay as described in *A Potter's Book* by Bernard Leach (1940) 47–53. Herbert Marwitz, "Zur griechischen Vasentechnik," *Jahreshefte des Osterreichischen archäologischen Institutes* Band XLV (1960) 209–263, refers to the aging of clay in China for as long as 100 years, and he even suggests that Attic potters might have aged their clay for a generation (p. 214). In China, the reason for the long aging was the fact that the clay was often a primary clay, stiff and difficult to work. The aging was done outdoors, turning it over every few months to allow the rain and frost to break down its structure and make it malleable. In some areas many years were needed before the clay could be thrown properly. In Attica, the situation was completely different, because the red clay is a secondary clay, malleable and ready to use soon after it comes from the clay pit. Aging for a few months helps it slightly, but it does not need to be weathered to soften its structure.

The malleability of clay and its ability to take a "set" is not clearly understood. Paul F. Kerr, "Quick Clay," *Scientific American* 209, no. 5 (November 1963) 132, describes the collapse of clays, the use of salt to stabilize them, and tannic acid to keep them fluid.

6 Translation by Helen McClees.

7 Lindsay Scott, "Pottery," *A History of Technology*, vol. I (1954) 376–378.

8 Adolf Rieth, *Die Entwicklung der Töpferscheibe* (1939), 10.

9 Brian A. Sparkes and Lucy Talcott, *Pots and Pans of Classical Athens* (1961). Brian A. Sparkes, "The Greek Kitchen," *The Journal of Hellenic Studies*, 82 (1962) pp. 122–137, pls IV-VIII.

10 Carl W. Blegen, John L. Caskey, Marion Rawson, and Jerome Sperling, *Troy*, vol. I part 1 (1950) 255.

The use of wheel-made pottery spread slowly by diffusion from the Near East to Europe and America. The following list of dates of its introduction to various areas is taken from "Rotary Motion" by V. Gordon Childe, *A History of Technology*, vol. I (1954) p. 203: Sumer 3250 ± 250 BC; Mediterranean coast of Syria and Palestine 3000 BC; Egypt 2750 BC; Crete 2000 BC; mainland Greece 1800 BC; South Italy 750 BC; upper Danube – upper Rhine basins 400 BC; southern England 50 BC; Scotland 400 AD; the Americas 1550 AD.

11 Gisela M. A. Richter, *The Craft of Athenian Pottery* (1923), 89–90. References to ancient authors are given, naming the following as the inventors of the potter's wheel: Talos, the son of Daedalus' sister; Anacharsis, the Scythian; Hyperbius, the Corinthian; and an unknown resident of Marathon. Coroebus, the Athenian, is said to have invented earthen pots.

12 Translation by Lang, Leaf and Myers.

13 See Introduction, note 8.

14 L. D. Caskey, *Geometry of Greek Vases* (1922).

15 *Hesperia*, XX, 1951, pl. 53b, no. 10 (Pyre no. 11).

16 In modern Mediterranean pottery practice, as observed by Roland Hampe and Adam Winter, lids are thrown right side up and then inverted and hollowed out.

Lids are studied by Dietrich von Bothmer, in "Lids By Andokides," *Berliner Museen*, 14 (1964) 38–41.

17 Translation by Helen McClees. The room should not be hot, cold, or drafty.

18 Roland Hampe and Adam Winter, *Bei Töpfern und Töpferinnen in Kreta Messenien und Zypern* (1962).

19 Translation by Helen McClees.

20 Translation by Helen McClees.

21 A description of the vase in ill. 110 and a list of representations of psykters on vases is given by Dietrich von Bothmer in the review of *Attic and South Italian Painted Vases at Haverford College* by Howard Comfort (1956) in *American Journal of Archaeology* 61 (1957) 309.

22 The various types of rhyta have been surveyed in *Attic Red-Figured Rhyta* by Herbert Hoffmann (1962).

23 Roland Hampe and Erika Simon, *Griechisches Leben im Spiegel der Kunst* (1959), 36, footnote 36.

24 Dietrich von Bothmer, *Ancient Art From New York Private Collections* (1961), 60, pls. 88, 92.

Cedric G. Boulter, "Graves in Lenormant Street, Athens," *Hesperia* XXXII, no. 2 (1963) 123, fig. 4 presents a cross-section drawing of a lekythos with an interior cup by the Thanatos Painter.

Joseph Veach Noble, "Some Trick Greek Vases," *Proceedings of the American Philosophical Society*, vol. 112, no. 6 (1968) 374–378, fig. 12–19 includes nineteen white-ground lekythoi with inner containers.

25 C. H. E. Haspels, *Attic Black-Figured Lekythoi* (1936) 176–7, pl. 51.

26 The ancient name for a pyxis may be kylichnis as proposed by Marjorie J. Milne, "Kylichnis," *American Journal of Archaeology*, 43 (1939) 247–254.

27 Herbert Hoffman, "Two Deer Heads from Apulia," *American Journal of Archaeology*, 64 (1960) 276–278, pls 77–78. Herbert Hoffman, *Tarentine Rhyta* (1966) p. 65, pl. 41, 3–6.

28 See Note 27, supra.

29 J. D. Beazley, *Attic Red-figure Vase-painters*, second edition (1963) 971, nos 6 and 7.

CHAPTER TWO: THE GREEK BLACK GLAZE

1 Dr Schumann in his original publication, *Berichte der deutschen keramischen Gesellschaft* 23 (1942) 408–26, suggested other deflocculants such as dregs of wine, urine and certain earths which have a strong character of decay. H. Marwitz, "Zur griechischen Vasentechnik," *Jahreshefte des Österreichischen archäologischen Institutes*, Band XLV (1960) 209–263 suggests that Attic potters aged the clay for a generation after treating it with urine or blood to help the bacterial action and defloculation. The process will work without the years of storage. Roland Hampe told me that he and Adam Winter could not defloculate the clay with urine. Neither could I. (See Chapter One, note 5.) Adam Winter in *Die Antike Glanztonkeramik*, Mainz (1978) presents a comprehensive treatment of the technology of the black glaze.

2 The process as described is the author's method of reproducing the ancient black and red ware. It has the advantage of being accomplished in a single firing and is uniform in results. Other methods have been proposed; one publication is P. O. A. L. Davies, "Red and Black Egyptian Pottery," *The Journal of*

Egyptian Archaeology, vol. 48 (1962) 19–24. He proposes two separate firings; the first as oxidizing, the second placing the inverted vases with their mouths in deep charcoal and ash. This was also proposed by A. Lucas, *Ancient Egyptian Materials and Industries*, fourth edition (1962) 377–381.

3 Marian H. Sagan has written a thesis, *The Pottery from Vasiliki* (1962), a copy of which is in the library of Bryn Mawr College, Bryn Mawr, Pennsylvania. It surveys the subject and includes a summary of my work on the technical process as described. The first theory for the origin of the spots was proposed by Richard B. Seager in "Excavations at Vasiliki, 1904," *Transactions of the Department of Archaeology, Free Museum of Science and Art, University of Pennsylvania*, vol. 1 (1904–1905) 216. He reported, "Exactly how this effect was obtained has not yet been satisfactorily explained, but possibly the vases were covered with paint and then put into a bed of coals which were heaped over them, the black patches being the effect of a live coal lying actually against the surface of the vase."

Charles F. Binns rejected Seager's idea and proposed that a carbonaceous pigment such as tar was painted on the unfired vase to form the spots during the firing. The burning tar was intended to reduce the iron in the clay and cause carbon smudging (Gisela M. A. Richter, *The Craft of Athenian Pottery* [1923] 45). In 1927 H. Frankfort stated, "Mr Seager was right in principle. . . . This regularity derives, of course, from the initial disposition of the fuel round the vase by the potter." He cited one vase as the unique exception to the rule. "[It] shows a pair of wavy lines on each side; but here the mottled effect is in itself at once less rich in shades, and I get the impression that the design is here executed with a bright burning branch" (*Studies in Early Pottery of the Near East*, II, Royal Anthropological Institute [1927] 91.) Mr F. O. Waage thought that the spots were produced by jets of air and gases streaming up through holes in a perforated floor of the kiln ("Notes on Mottled Vases," *American Journal of Archaeology* 37 [1933] 405).

4 Other examples, including a sixth century BC specimen from Gordion, are given in Marie Farnsworth and Ivor Simmons, "Coloring Agents for Greek Glazes," *American Journal of Archaeology*, 67 (1963) 389–96, pls 87–8. See also François Schweizer and Anne Rinuy, "Manganese Black as an Etruscan Pigment," *Studies In Conservation*, 27 (1982) 118–123.

5 The formula given in the metric system is: $\frac{1}{2}$ liter distilled water; $2\frac{1}{2}$ grams Calgon [sodium hexametaphosphate $(NaPO_3)_6$], 115 grams damp Attic clay.

The deflocculating agent used by the ancient Attic potters may have been potash (potassium carbonate, K_2CO_3) produced by soaking wood ashes in water. Potash is completely satisfactory in the preparation of the black glaze.

6 Mavis Bimson, "The Technique of Greek Black and Terra Sigillata Red," *The Antiquaries Journal* 36 (1956) 200–204.

7 F. Oberlies and N. Köppen, "Untersuchungen an Terra Sigillata und griechischen Vasen," *Berichte der deutschen keramischen Gesellschaft* 30 (1953) 102–110. Also by the same authors in the same publication: "Tonüberzüge, ein Veredlungsverfahren für Keramiken" 31 (1954) 287–301; "Untersuchungen an griechischen Gefässfragmenten aus verschiedenen Jahrhunderten v. Chr." 39 (1962) 19–31.

8 A study by U. Hofmann, "The Chemical Basis of Ancient Greek Vase Painting," *Angewandte Chemie*, 1 (1962) 341–350, illustrates electron micrographs of various surfaces of ancient Greek black glaze. Fig. 8 compares the surface of the smooth, sintered black glaze and the coarse, porous red clay body.

9 In pre-Columbian times several American Pueblo Indian tribes, among them the Santa Clara of New Mexico, invented a plain black pottery resembling Etruscan bucchero ware. The vases were hand-formed from a red iron-bearing clay without the use of a potter's wheel. A kiln was not used in the firing. Probably the vases were piled on the ground and a fire built over them. After the fire reached its greatest intensity it was partially smothered by covering it with animal dung. This created a great amount of smoke and changed the firing from oxidizing to reducing conditions and also caused carbon smudging. The fire was allowed to die out without changing back to a reoxidizing condition. The resulting pottery was completely black.

In 1918–19 Julian and Maria Martinez at the San Ildefonso Pueblo in New Mexico accidentally invented a black pottery which duplicated the Santa Clara type, but they decorated their pottery with dull black designs over the shiny surface of the balance of the vase. After the vase was formed, it was burnished. Then designs were drawn on it with a clay slip which produced a matte surface. The ware was subjected to an oxidizing and then a reducing firing that achieved dull matte black designs in contrast to the lustrous black of the surface of the vase. This is the "black on black" pottery which is now produced by the entire San Ildefonso Pueblo.

The observation of primitive or peasant potters is a valid and fruitful pursuit. They are facing the same problems as the ancient potters, and often they preserve unchanged work patterns and techniques. Such studies are in the books by Roland Hampe and Adam Winter, *Bei Töpfern und Töpferinnen in Kreta Messenien und Zypern* (1962), and *Bei Töpfern und Zieglern in Süditalien Sizilien und Griechenland* (1965).

10 These techniques are discussed in the following publications: Mavis Bimson, "The Technique of Greek Black and Terra Sigillata Red," *The Antiquaries Journal* 36 (1956) 200–204, pl. XIV; C. R.

Amberg, "Terra Sigillata, Forgotten Finish," *Ceramic Industry*, 51 (1948) 77; J. A. Stanfield and Grace Simpson, *Central Gaulish Potters* (1958); R. J. Charleston, *Roman Pottery* (1955).

11 Anna O. Shepard, *Plumbate, A Mesoamerican Trade Ware* (1948) 91–99.

12 C. R. Amberg, "Terra Sigillata, Forgotten Finish," *Ceramic Industry*, 51 (1948) 77.

CHAPTER THREE: DECORATING THE VASES

1 Dietrich von Bothmer, *Corpus Vasorum Antiquorum, The Metropolitan Museum of Art*, Fascicule 3 [U.S.A. fascicule 12] (1963) "Attic Black-figured Amphorae," 4, 5 pls 6, 7. Dietrich von Bothmer, *The Amasis Painter and His World* (1985), 70–73.

2 The chronology of Attic black-figure and red-figure pottery and the study of the artists who produced it are vast fields of investigation that lie outside the scope of this book. The following three works survey these fields: J. D. Beazley, *The Development of Attic Black-Figure* (1951); Gisela M. A. Richter, *Attic Red-Figured Vases: a Survey* (1946); revised edition (1958); R. M. Cook, *Greek Painted Pottery* (1960).

3 Sketch lines on numerous vases are illustrated in A. Furtwängler and K. Reichhold, *Griechische Vasenmalerei* (1900–1932). P.E. Corbett, "Preliminary Sketch In Greek Vase-Painting," *The Journal of Hellenic Studies* 85 (1965), p. 16–28 pls I–XV.

4 Observed by Fritz Eichler, *Corpus Vasorum Antiquorum*, Wien, Kunsthistorisches Museum, Band I (1951) 9, pl. 2, no. 3691, Attic red-figure kylix by the Epidromos Painter.

5 Attic kylix in the manner of the Antiphon Painter, in The Metropolitan Museum of Art, acc. no. 07.286.48, Rogers Fund. J. D. Beazley, *American Journal of Archaeology* 57 (1953) 41, review of *CVA*, Wien, Band I.

6 Pair of Attic kylikes, by Aristophanes, in the Museum of Fine Arts, Boston, acc. nos. 00.344, 00.345. L. D. Caskey and J. D. Beazley, *Attic Vase Paintings in the Museum of Fine Arts, Boston*, Part III (1963) 83–87, nos 171, 172, pls CIII–CV.

7 J. D. Beazley, *Attic Red-figure Vase-painters* second edition (1963) 4, no. 12. L. D. Caskey and J. D. Beazley, *Attic Vase Paintings in the Museum of Fine Arts, Boston*, Part III (1963) 7, 8, no. 115, pls LXV, LXVII.

8 J. D. Beazley, *Attic Black-figure Vase-painters* (1956) 482, no. 10.

9 Attic calyx krater, by the Kleophrades Painter, in The Metropolitan Museum of Art, acc. no. 08.258.58, Rogers Fund. Gisela M. A. Richter and Lindsley F. Hall, *Red-Figured Athenian Vases In The Metropolitan Museum of Art* (1936) 35, pl. 12.

10 Excellent examples of representations of Greek potters and painters at work are given in Gisela M. A. Richter, *The Craft of Athenian Pottery* (1923).

11 This vase has been illustrated several times since its first publication in 1876 (*Annali dell'Instituto* 1876, pl. D, E). The best description of this vase by the Leningrad Painter appears in J. D. Beazley, "Potter and Painter in Ancient Athens" *Proceedings of the British Academy* 30 (1946) 97–99. See also this Introduction, note 9.

In vol. LXXXI (1961) *The Journal of Hellenic Studies* "The Caputi Hydria," 73–75, pls VI–VII, Richard Green has advanced the theory that the four vase decorators shown on the hydria by the Leningrad Painter are working on metal vases rather than pottery as had previously been assumed. This is an intriguing suggestion but unfortunately it does not withstand detailed examination.

The scene is an idealized representation of a vase-painter's workshop. Athena and two nikai approach to crown with laurel the heads of the three male vase-painters, apparently as a reward for the excellence of their work. The neatly draped clothing of the human figures surely is not typical of their daily work clothes. The chair and table used by the master painter is of extreme delicacy and of a far higher quality than the rude stools customarily used in the shop. Even the pots themselves are larger or finer than normal, particularly the huge kantharos being decorated by the master painter. In short, the entire studio has been rendered in an idealized manner befitting the visit of Athena, patron goddess of the craftsmen. It is important to note that Athena, patron of potters, is present rather than Hephaistos who was associated with metal working.

Despite this idealization, some realistic and practical details of the work are observed. The master craftsman balances the kantharos on his lap and the painter working on the calyx krater cushions it on a pad. At the time of decorating, the clay vessels were only partially dry and leather-hard. If the clay were too damp, the vase would slump, and if too dry it would take the glaze badly causing it to flake. In fact, a vase in the leather-hard state was stronger than when completely dry. Tests with modern reproductions of ancient vases demonstrate that the cohesive quality of Attic clay allowed a leather-hard vase to be handled as shown on this hydria. When the vases were completely dry they were stacked in the kiln by nesting one inside another, as indicated by the oinochoe inside the kantharos on the floor. Actually, this particular nesting is top heavy and would be undesirable for either clay or metal vases, and apparently was done only to fill the space between the master painter and Athena.

The scene takes place on a shady porch as is shown by the elevated floor on which the woman painter works. Over her head two fired vases hang on the wall. Nowhere do we see metal working tools, no casting equipment, no hammers and forms for repoussé work, and no gravers for the final engraving and chasing of metal vases. Instead, the only tools we see are brushes and glaze pots. Each of the four painters wields a brush, and all of their glaze pots are visible except the woman's.

Mr Green has suggested that the painters are applying either an adhesive base for gold leaf or an amalgam of gold and mercury in order to create gilded decoration on metal vases. If gold leaf gilding were being employed, an adhesive of either honey or resin would be used and only a single cup would be required, whereas two of the painters have two cups. The gold leaf would have to be pressed onto the adhesive surface while it was still tacky and then burnished. However, gold leaf and burnishing tools are not in evidence. Mercury gilding also would have required only one cup.

In summary, there is no evidence that the painters on this hydria are working on metal vases; instead, they are plying their craft of decorating unfired pottery with the Greek black glaze.

12 J. D. Beazley, *Attic Red-figure Vase-painters* second edition (1963) 197; no.3; Dietrich von Bothmer, *Bulletin of The Metropolitan Museum of Art* 15:7 (March 1957) 165–180 and color cover.

13 J. D. Beazley, *Attic Red-figure Vase-painters* second edition (1963) 342, no. 19. L. D. Caskey and J. D. Beazley, *Attic Vase Paintings in the Museum of Fine Arts, Boston*, Part III (1963) 43, 44, no. 146, pl. LXXXI, 1. This vase also demonstrates the way a vase-painter held a kylix while painting it. Rarely is the scene in the tondo oriented so that when the handles are horizontal the scene is properly vertical. Often when the scene is viewed correctly the handles are at a "two o'clock, eight o'clock" position. Dietrich von Bothmer has pointed out that this position allowed the lower handle to steady the cup while painting. When a cup hung on its peg in the wall only the exterior could be seen, and the orientation of the tondo drawing was not important.

Note also that the painter on this kylix holds his brush differently than the four vase-painters on the hydria in the Torno collection. Both methods were in use.

14 One has only to try a fine brush, pen, feather, etc. with the heavy glaze matter to realize the problem in trying to make such a heavy substance flow of its own accord. If glaze matter is not available for a test, use black oil paint thickened enough to form a line in relief.

The equivalent of a modern drafting pen made with a quill as proposed by Winter will work for only short crude lines and does not reproduce the delicacy and length of the relief lines found on Attic vases. Adam Winter, "Die Technik des griechischen Töpfers in ihren Grundlagen" in *Technische Beiträge zur Archäologie*, Mainz (1959).

Karl Reichhold, *Skizzenbuch griechischer Meister* (1919) reviews the early theories about the relief line.

15 G. Roger Edwards of The University Museum in Philadelphia called my attention to the relationship of West Slope ware to the Attic relief line and to the Barbotine technique.

Professor Robert Zahn was the first to describe accurately the production of Barbotine ware, "Glasierter Tonbecher im Berliner Antiquarium," *Winckemannsprogramm der Archaeologischen Gesellschaft zu Berlin* (1923), footnote no. 5. He stated that he recognized the extruded technique because he was the son of a pastry chef and had often watched his father decorate cakes with frosting in a similar manner.

16 C. T. Seltman, *Athens, Its History and Coinage Before the Persian Invasion* (1924) 13.

17 For various references to the ancient sources of ocher, see Marie Farnsworth and Harriet Wisely, "Fifth Century Intentional Red Glaze," *American Journal of Archaeology* 62 (1958) 169–170.

18 The white ground on lekythoi often had a creamy tone. This was apparently deliberate because added white applied to the same lekythoi is whiter in shade, making a chalky white contrast with the creamy white ground. The added white used on black-figure loutrophoroi was tinted a creamy shade. In Attic black-figure, white was usually used to portray women's faces but when painting on white-ground vases this did not yield sufficient contrast; therefore, the women's faces were painted black.

Occasionally, vase-painters made experimental vases which do not correspond to the conventional techniques as herein discussed. One example is an amphora in the Louvre (F203) by the Andokides Painter, which depicts Amazons. To portray their flesh as white, the painter coated the panels with a white background and painted around the figures with black glaze on top of the white slip. J. D. Beazley, *Attic Red-figure Vase-painters* second edition (1963) 4, no. 13; Dietrich von Bothmer, *Amazons in Greek Art* (1957) 149, no. 34, 153–154.

19 A. D. Ure, "Krokotos and White Heron," *Journal of Hellenic Studies* 75 (1955) 90–103.

20 Dietrich von Bothmer, *Amazons in Greek Art* (1957) 95, no. 59, discussed on p. 96, ill. pl. LXI, no. 3, Munich 2030 (a black-figured eye-cup).

21 Michael Vickers, "Two More Rattling Cups," *American Journal of Archaeology* 78, (1974) 429–31, pl. 88.

22 Gisela M. A. Richter, *Attic Red-Figured Vases: a Survey* (1958) 31.

23 Marie Farnsworth and Harriet Wisely, "Fifth Century Intentional Red Glaze," *American Journal of Archaeology* 62 (1958) 165–173, pl. 36 and color plate.

24 R. A. Higgins, "The Polychrome Decoration of Greek Terracottas," *Studies In Conservation* 15 (1970), 272–277 reports the following pigments used. Red is red ocher (hematite) or, less commonly, vermilion (cinnabar). Pink is a mixture of red ocher and chalk before 330 BC, after that time it was rose

madder, a natural dye made from the root of a plant. Yellow is yellow ocher. Blue is Egyptian blue, or blue frit made with silica, copper, chalk, and natron. Green is malachite, an ore of copper. Black is either soot or bitumen. White is either chalk or gypsum. A shiny effect was not due to a glaze but was obtained by burnishing. All of the pigments must have been put on after firing with a binder such as white of egg, as these pigments are unstable at the temperature required for firing. These tests were conducted in the Research Laboratory of the British Museum by A. E. Werner and M. Bimson.

25 The Centuripe ware of Southern Italy of the third century BC also was painted with unfired colors over a white clay slip. The colors tend to flake and fade easily.

26 B. A. Sparkes, "Black Perseus," *Antike Kunst* 11, 1 (1968), 3–16, pls 1–8.

27 The use of stamps made from silver or gold vases was later extensively utilized in the manufacture of molds for the mass production of "Megarian," "Pergamene" and Arretine pottery. Impressions were made by pressing soft clay against individual figures or patterns on the metal vase and, after drying, these small pieces were fired. The stamps were produced by putting soft clay in the fired impressions. After the stamps were fired, they could be used in various combinations to create the designs in the molds. A mold was made by forming a heavy clay bowl on the potter's wheel and the stamps were impressed on the inside. Connecting lines and details were added freehand. The impressed bowl was then fired and used as a mold. It was mounted on a potter's wheel and the final bowl was formed inside the mold by spinning the clay over the entire inside surface. When the inside bowl dried, it shrank away from the mold and could be readily removed. Handles and a foot were added if desired. After drying, the bowl was glazed and fired. For illustrations of Arretine stamps, molds, and vases refer to *Corpus Vasorum Antiquorum, USA, fascicule 9, The Metropolitan Museum of Art, fascicule 1* (1943) by Christine Alexander.

28 It is interesting to note that this is the same process employed by Josiah Wedgwood in producing his pottery jasper ware copies of the Portland vase starting in 1790. The original Roman vase had been carved in dark blue and white cameo glass.

29 Gisela M. A. Richter, *Attic Red-Figured Vases: a survey* (1958) 14–23.

CHAPTER FOUR: FIRING THE VASES

1 This often happens with modern pottery made by the Indians of the pueblos of the American South-west, much to the chagrin of the tourists who have purchased it.

2 Refer to Appendix III for the Greek text and a fuller discussion of it.

3 See Introduction, note 8.

4 Humfry Payne, *Necrocorinthia* (1931) 117, note 2. *Gazette archéologique*, VI, 105.

5 *Antike Denkmaeler*, I, pl. 8, no. 12. Humfry Payne, *Necrocorinthia* (1931) 117, note 2.

6 Adam Winter, "Die Technik des griechischen Töpfers in ihren Grundlagen," in *Technische Beiträge zur Archäologie*, Mainz (1959). Contains a diagram of an ancient kiln.

7 *Antike Denkmaeler*, I, pl. 8, no. 4. Humfry Payne, *Necrocorinthia* (1931) 117, note 2.
Note the use of the mouth of a broken amphora as a vent at the top of the kiln. The use of broken vases for this purpose continues in the Mediterranean area today.

8 *Antike Denkmaeler*, I, pl. 8, no. 21. Humfry Payne, *Necrocorinthia* (1931) 117, note 2.

9 *Antike Denkmaeler*, I, pl. 8, no. 22.

10 *Antike Denkmaeler*, I, pl. 8, no. 26.

11 *Antike Denkmaeler*, I, pl. 8, no. 19b. The other side of the pinax is shown in 19a. Humfry Payne, *Necrocorinthia* (1931) 117, note 2. Ninina Cuomo Di Caprio, "Pottery Kilns on Pinakes from Corinth," in *Ancient Greek and Related Pottery* (1984) 72–82. In figs 1–18 all of these pinakes are illustrated.

12 R. M. Cook, "The 'Double Stoking Tunnel' of Greek Kilns," in *The Annual of The British School of Archaeology at Athens* 56 (1961) 64–67, pl. 7. The estimate that the complete pinax was at least twice as large as the preserved fragment is based on the drawing on the other side of the plaque. It depicts a man and the hind part of a huge boar. The plaque must have been at least twice as large in order to provide space for the drawing of a complete animal. This would provide the additional space on the kiln side for the tunnel and potter. Also, included in the article is a list of the locations of more than fifty ancient Greek kilns.
Other kilns including recent finds in Russia are given by Juliusz Ziomecki, "Die keramischen Techniken im antiken Griechenland," *Raggi: Zeitschrift für Kunstgeschichte und Archäologie*, Heft ½, 1964, p. 27. ff. 93.

13 Roland Hampe reported to me that he and Adam Winter observed in the town of Camerota, Provincia di Salerno in Southern Italy, that it was the practice to place unfired pots behind the pillar in the firing pit as shown in this pinax. Therefore, the boat-shaped object may be another vase being fired.

14 Marie Farnsworth, "Draw Pieces as Aids to Correct Firing," *American Journal of Archaeology* 64 (1960) 72–75, pl. 16.

15 Marie Farnsworth, "Draw Pieces as Aids to Correct Firing," *American Journal of Archaeology* 64 (1960) 75, pl. 16, H and I. Draw pieces are also illustrated in *Corpus Vasorum Antiquoram*, Bonn. pl. 19,3; pl. 38,1,2; and P. Hartwig, "Die Anwendung der Federfahne bei den griechischen Vasenmalern," *Jahrbuch*

des Kaiserlich Deutschen Archäologischen Instituts 14 (1899) 165–166.

16 Oliver S. Tonks, "Experiments with the Black Glaze on Greek Vases," *American Journal of Archaeology* 12 (1908) 421.

17 At 950°C. the interior of the kiln, including the vases, glows with an incandescent yellow-white light. It is impossible to see if the vases are blackened as proposed by C. P. T. Naude, "The Glaze Technique of the Attic Vase," *Acta Classica* 2 (1959). The vases are emitting light, and resemble brightly glowing coals on a hearth. The temperature even can be determined by judging the intensity of the radiant energy striking the face.

18 Charles F. Binns and A. D. Fraser, "The Genesis of the Greek Black Glaze," *American Journal of Archaeology* 33 (1929) 7.

19 In all of the tests, I used a small electric kiln. Temperatures were gauged by the use of pyrometric cones rather than by a pyrometer. The cones have the advantage of indicating the effect of prolonged heat as well as the temperature and therefore measure the effect of the firing of the pottery more closely.

20 J. P. Roberts has been determining firing temperatures based on a system described by F. H. Norton, *Refractories* third edition (1949) 484, and has reported his findings in two articles: "Some Experiments on Romano-British Colour-Coated Ware" and "Determination of the Firing Temperature of Ancient Pottery by Measurement of Thermal Expansion," both in *Archaeometry* 6 (1964). A small sample of pottery is heated slowly under controlled conditions and its expansion is measured precisely. The expansion continues until the sample reaches its original firing temperature. At that point, vitrification of the clay is resumed and the sample starts to shrink, as is normal in vitrification. The temperature at the start of the shrinkage is the ancient firing temperature. In effect, the modern firing continues the vitrification process from where it was stopped at the height of the ancient firing. Accuracy to ± 20°C. is claimed.

The problems of the construction and operation of a kiln somewhat similar to the Greek type are discussed in the following articles: B. R. Hartley, "The Firing of Kilns of Romano-British Type: Archaeological Notes," *Archaeometry*, 4 (1961) 1–3. P. Mayes, "The Firing of a Pottery Kiln of a Romano-British Type at Boston, Lincs." *Ibid.*, 4–30. Appendices: I: J. P. Roberts, "Temperature Measurements;" II: D. White and A. White, "Gas Analysis;" III: G. H. Weaver, "Magnetic Dating Measurements;" IV: M. J. Aitken, "Measurement of the Magnetic Anomaly." Philip Mayes, "The Firing of a Second Pottery Kiln of Romano-British Type at Boston, Lincolnshire," *Archaeometry*, 5 (1962) 80–92. Appendices: I: J. P. Roberts, "Temperature Measurements;" II: A. E. White and D. White, "Gas Analysis." G. H. Weaver, "Archaeomagnetic Measurements on the

Second Boston Experimental Kiln," *Ibid.*, 93–107.

21 Marie Farnsworth, "Types of Greek Glaze Failure," in *Archaeology* 12 (1959) 242–250.

22 See note 21, supra. This process of dissolving iron in a glaze was used to produce the light green color in Chinese celadon ware.

23 Attic pelike, by the Berlin Painter in the Kunsthistorisches Museum in Vienna, no. 3725 (ex Oest. Mus. 333). Fritz Eichler, *Corpus Vasorum Antiquorum*, Wien, fasc. 2. III, 1, pls. 68, 69, p. 17. "Ghosts" are not limited to Attic pottery; they occur frequently on South Italian and Cypriot vases.

CHAPTER FIVE: CONCLUSION

1 Ocher was used only after the second generation of black-figure painters.

2 Sometimes, in panel amphorae or column kraters with the pictures in panels, or hydriai, the rest of the vase is painted black before the design on the panel is begun.

APPENDIX I

1 J. D. Beazley, *Attic Black-figured Vase-painters* (1956) and *Attic Red-figured Vase-painters* (1942), second edition (1963), *Paralipomena* (1971).

2 M. J. Aitken, *Physics and Archaeology* (1961) sets forth various uses of science in archaeological work. Additional information is given in *The Application of Quantitative Methods in Archaeology*, edited by R. F. Heizer and S. F. Cook (1960) in the section "The Quantitative Study of Ceramic Materials," by F. R. Matson.

3 F. Oberlies and N. Köppen, "Untersuchungen an griechischen Gefässfragmenten aus verschiedenen Jahrhunderten v. Chr.," *Berichte der deutschen keramischen Gesellschaft* 39 (1962) 19–31.

4 It is interesting to note that during the seventh century BC Corinth used a great deal of black glaze and Athens very little. By the end of the seventh century, both the Corinthian style and the black glaze were imitated by Athenian potters.

5 J. D. Beazley, *Attic Black-figured Vase-painters* (1956) 228.

6 H. W. Catling, A. E. Blin-Stoyle, and E. E. Richards, "Spectrographic Analysis of Mycenaean and Minoan Pottery," *Archaeometry* 4 (1961) 31–38, presents the results of the analysis of about 200 sherds.

7 E. V. Sayre and R. W. Dodson, "Neutron Activation Study of Mediterranean Potsherds," *American Journal of Archaeology* 61 (1957) 35–41.

Dominique Fillieres, Garman Harbottle and Edward V. Sayre, "Neutron Activation Study of Figurines, Pottery and Workshop Materials from the Athenian Agora, Greece," *Journal of Field Archaeology* 10 (1983) 55–69.

R. E. Jones, "Greek Potters' Clays: Questions of

Selection, Availability and Adaption," *Ancient Greek and Related Pottery* (1984) 21–30.

8 Anna O. Shepard, *Ceramics for the Archaeologist* (1956) 378–384.

9 Marie Farnsworth, "Greek Pottery: A Mineralogical Study," *American Journal of Archaeology* 68 (1964) 221–228, pls 65–68; includes a geologic map and a series of microscopic photographs of clay bodies.

Marie Farnsworth, "Corinthian Pottery: Technical Studies," *American Journal of Archaeology* 74 (1970) 9–20, pl. 1–2.

10 There is a large body of literature on the subject of forgeries, but I have found that one of the most interesting articles is by Hans Tietze, "The Psychology and Aesthetics of Forgery in Art," *Metropolitan Museum Studies*, vol. v, part 1, June 1934.

11 Refer to Chapter Two, *"The Greek Black Glaze."*

12 James J. Rorimer, *Ultra-Violet Rays and Their Use in the Examination of Works of Art* (1931).

13 Murray Pease, "Two Bowls In One," *The Metropolitan Museum of Art Bulletin*, vol. xvi, No. 8, April 1958, 236–240.

14 J. V. Noble, "The Technique of Attic Vase-Painting," *American Journal of Archaeology* 64 (1960) 311.

Dietrich von Bothmer and Joseph V. Noble, "An Inquiry Into the Forgery of the Etruscan Terracotta Warriors in The Metropolitan Museum of Art," in *The Metropolitan Museum of Art Papers* No. 11 (1961). The three "Etruscan" Terracotta Warriors which were covered with a black glaze were under study for over forty years. Their huge size, structure, and the lack of similar examples, had made them famous and controversial. After comparative spectrographic analyses were made, I found that manganese, a coloring agent not often used in classical times, was used to produce the imitation of the ancient black glaze, thus proving that they were colossal forgeries. Analyses of genuine and forged terracottas are presented including those made of the terracotta warriors and the Castellani sarcophagus. In addition to describing the spectrographic test, a temperature test is given. In this rapid and simple test a flake of black glaze is taken from an inconspicuous spot on the suspected vase and heated to a temperature of 1050°C. If the glaze is correct it will reoxidize to a red color, and if it is false, and made from a mineral pigment such as manganese, it will remain black. This test can prove a vase a forgery, but it does not prove the antiquity of the piece, because the new generation of forgers are using the correct formula for the black glaze as given in this book.

APPENDIX II

1 Mary B. Moore, "A Neck Amphora in the Collection of Walter Bareiss, I. The Painter," *American Journal of Archaeology* 76 (1972) 1–9, pls 1–6, and Dietrich von Bothmer, "II. The Ancient Repairs," 9–11, pls 1–6.

2 Hansjörg Bloesch, "Stout and Slender in the Late Archaic Period," *Journal of Hellenic Studies* 71 (1951) 30.

3 The back of a terracotta plaque from the volute of an Apulian krater owned by David H. Swingler was coated with a black tar-like material. I had the conservation laboratory of The J. Paul Getty Museum test it, and they discovered that the substance was natural asphalt.

4 William J. Young of the Museum of Fine Arts, Boston, has informed me of an unusual procedure that he used in cleaning the Attic red-figured bell krater by the Pan Painter, acc. no. 10.185. The vase had a heavy encrustation of silica; under it, on the surface of the vase, was a thin layer of a lime deposit. He refired the vase at a temperature of about 900°C., thereby destroying the lime layer, which then allowed the silica layer to be removed easily. Refiring vases with only the silica encrustation has not been successful in loosening the deposit. In rare cases a black deposit of manganese occurs and requires special treatment. V. Daniels, "Manganese-Containing Stains on Excavated Pottery Sherds," *MASCA Journal* 1 (1981) 230–231.

5 The "Appendix" by Dietrich von Bothmer of Marie Farnsworth and Harriet Wisely's article "Fifth Century Intentional Red Glaze" in *American Journal of Archaeology* 62 (1958) 173, pl. 37, contains good illustrations of a vase before and after refiring. Joseph Veach Noble, "Refiring Greek Vases," *American Journal of Archaeology* 89 (1985) 515–516.

6 Duco Cement or Ambroid Cement are two satisfactory products. The permanent type of bond such as those created by the epoxy resins should not be used because there may be a need to take the vase apart at a future date.

Animal glue or shellac is preferred by some restorers since they set more slowly and allow more time for adjusting the fit of the fragments.

7 Hansjörg Bloesch, "Conseils pour photographier les vases grecs," *Colloque International Sur Le Corpus Vasorum Antiquorum* (1956) 31–33.

8 The distracting highlights on the shiny black glaze surface were a difficult problem to overcome. For many years, the best solution was that employed by Professor Ernst Langlotz who used large silk screens over the photographic lights to create a complete diffusion of the highlights. In the 1930s Edwin H. Land invented a process of imbedding a light polarizing material in sheets of clear plastic. This was immediately adopted by photographers who found that if a Polaroid screen were placed over the light source, and another over the lens, highlights could be eliminated by canceling the polarized reflections.

Sources of Illustrations

Art, acc. no. 56.171.45, Fletcher Fund.

103 Attic volute krater, The Metropolitan Museum of Art, acc. no. 07.286.84, Rogers Fund.

104 Attic calyx krater, The Metropolitan Museum of Art, acc. no. 56.171.48, Fletcher Fund.

105 Attic bell krater, The Metropolitan Museum of Art, acc. no. 28.57.23, Fletcher Fund.

106 Attic stamnos, The Metropolitan Museum of Art, acc. no. 21.88.3, Rogers Fund.

107 Attic stamnos, The Metropolitan Museum of Art, acc. no. 41.162.20, Rogers Fund.

108 Attic lebes, The Metropolitan Museum of Art, acc. no. 07.286.71, Rogers Fund.

109 Attic stamnos, Musées Royaux, Brussels, no. A 717.

110 Attic lekythos, Haverford College, Pennsylvania.

111 Attic psykter, The Metropolitan Museum of Art, acc. no. 60.11.6, Rogers Fund.

112 Attic kylix, The Metropolitan Museum of Art, acc. no. 06.1021.188, Rogers Fund.

113 Attic oinochoe, The Metropolitan Museum of Art, acc. no. 22.139.32, Rogers Fund.

114 Attic oinochoe, The Metropolitan Museum of Art, acc. no. 23.160.55, Rogers Fund.

115 Attic kyathos, The Metropolitan Museum of Art, acc. no. 24.97.8, Fletcher Fund.

116 Attic kylix in the collection of the author, Tampa Museum of Art, acc. no. 86.87

117 Attic kylix, The Metropolitan Museum of Art, acc. no. 56.171.62, Fletcher Fund.

118 Attic kylix, The Metropolitan Museum of Art, acc. no. 56.171.34, Fletcher Fund.

119 Attic kylix, The Metropolitan Museum of Art, acc. no. 06.1097, Rogers Fund.

120 Attic kylix, The Metropolitan Museum of Art, acc. no. 06.1021.167, Rogers Fund.

121 Attic kantharos, Museum of Fine Arts, Boston, acc. no. 00.334, Pierce Fund.

122 Attic oinochoe, Museum of Fine Arts, Boston, acc. no. 13.74, Bigelow Collection.

123 Attic black glazed and gilded kantharos, The J. Paul Getty Museum, acc. no. 82.AE.152.

124 Attic kylix, The Metropolitan Museum of Art, acc. no. 21.88.150, Rogers Fund.

125 Attic skyphos, The Metropolitan Museum of Art, acc. no. 56.171.59, Fletcher Fund.

126 Attic bell krater, Kunsthistorisches Museum, Vienna, no. 910.

127 Attic rhyton, The Metropolitan Museum of Art, acc. no. 06.1021.203, Rogers Fund.

128 Attic pelike, The Metropolitan Museum of Art, acc. no. 56.171.44, Fletcher Fund.

129 Attic phiale, Museum of Fine Arts, Boston, acc. no. 97.371, Perkins Collection.

130 Attic plate, The Metropolitan Museum of Art, acc. no. 41.162.55, Rogers Fund.

131 Attic lekythos, The Metropolitan Museum of Art, acc. no. 23.160.38, Rogers Fund.

132 Attic lekythos in the collection of the author, Tampa Museum of Art, acc. no. 86.79.

133 Attic lekythos, The Metropolitan Museum of Art, acc. no. 75.2.10. Gift of Samuel G. Ward.

134 Attic lekythos, The Metropolitan Museum of Art, acc. no. 25.78.2, Fletcher Fund.

135 Attic lekythos, The Metropolitan Museum of Art, acc. no. 30.11.8, Fletcher Fund.

136–38 Attic lekythos in the collection of the author, Tampa Museum of Art, acc. no. 86.79.

139 Attic aryballos, The Metropolitan Museum of Art, acc. no. 26.49, funds from various donors.

140 Attic aryballos, The Metropolitan Museum of Art, acc. no. 06.1021.112, Rogers Fund.

141 Attic calyx krater, Staatliche Museen, East Berlin, no. 2180.

142 Attic alabastron, The Metropolitan Museum of Art, acc. no. 08.258.27, Rogers Fund.

143 Attic lekythos, The Metropolitan Museum of Art, acc. no. 08.258.17, Rogers Fund.

144 Attic plemochoe, The Metropolitan Museum of Art, acc. no. 07.286.46, A and B, Rogers Fund.

145 Attic lekythos, The Metropolitan Museum of Art, acc. no. 30.11.8, Fletcher Fund.

146 Attic pyxis, The Metropolitan Museum of Art, acc. no. 07.286.36, Rogers Fund.

147 Attic pyxis, The Metropolitan Museum of Art, acc. no. 06.1021.120, Rogers Fund.

148 Attic lebes gamikos, Hermitage Museum, Leningrad, no. 15592.

149 Attic lekanis, The Metropolitan Museum of Art, acc. no. 17.230.42, A and B, Rogers Fund.

150 Attic red-figured lebes gamikos, Hermitage Museum, Leningrad, no. 15592.

151 Attic lebes gamikos, The Metropolitan Museum of Art, acc. no. 07.286.35, Rogers Fund.

152 Attic onos, National Museum, Athens, no. 1629.

153 See ill. 151.

154 Attic loutrophoros, The Metropolitan Museum of Art, acc. no. 27.228, funds from various donors.

155 Attic loutrophoros hydria, Louvre, no. MN 558.

156 See ill. 154.

157 Apulian patrix, The Metropolitan Museum of Art, acc. no. 10.210.124, Rogers Fund.

158 Apulian rhyton, The Metropolitan Museum of Art, acc. no. 03.3.2, Rogers Fund.

159 Attic kantharos, The Metropolitan Museum of Art, acc. no. 41.162.14, Rogers Fund.

160 Askos at the top, collection of the author, Tampa Museum of Art, acc. no. 86.96. Askos at the bottom, The Metropolitan Museum of Art, acc. no. 23.160.57, Rogers Fund.

161 Egyptian predynastic pottery, The Metropolitan Museum of Art. Left to right: acc. nos. 08.202.50, Rogers Fund; 99.4.111, Gift of the Egyptian Exploration Fund; 13.182.8, Rogers Fund.

162 Vase from Vasiliki, The Metropolitan Museum of Art, acc. no. 07.232.14, Gift of the American Exploration Society.

163 Attic red clay.

164, 165 Modern Attic black glaze material.

Index

Numbers in *italic* refer to the illustrations
Numbers in brackets, e.g., 202(3), refer to the number of the note on the page given